CRUSHING
CORPORATE

THE INTENTIONAL PURSUIT OF
SUCCESSFUL ENTREPRENEURSHIP
THROUGH INTRAPRENEURSHIP

Yoli Chisholm

CrushingCorporate.com

Yoli Chisholm / Crushing Corporate
15127 NE 24th St #452
Redmond, WA
www.crushingcorporate.com

Ordering Information:
Quantity sales. Special discounts are available on quantity purchases by corporations, associations, and others. For details, contact the "Special Sales Department" at the address above.

Crushing Corporate/ Yoli Chisholm. —1st ed.
ISBN 978-0-692-84824-1

Contents

*This book is dedicated to the bravest people I know
Zolile Thando Ngcakani and Pulane Fikile Ngcakani
who have crossed seas, learned many languages,
lived amongst many cultures and navigated
many worlds with the spirit of brave explorers.
It is an honor to be your daughter and I thank you
for sparking the adventurer in me.
To Zenyshia, Ayanda and Zanele, may you bravely
seek your path and take comfort in the fact
that you have an army of kin at the ready.*

You learn how to cut tress down by cutting them down.
— African Proverb

Knowing is not enough; we must apply. Willing is not enough; we must do.
--Johann Wolfgang von Goethe

Is 10% the best we can do?

I start every video on crushingcorporate.com with **"Hi my name is Yoli Chisholm and it's my objective to change your perspective"** This book is no different, it is my objective to change your perspective about working in a corporation. It finally crystallized for me why I wanted to write this book when I attended one of the best conferences I had ever been to in my whole career. I go to many conferences but this one was unique because unlike most of the professional conferences I go to, almost everyone in attendance was on a journey to starting their own business. Usually I am surrounded by professionals in my field of marketing or by people who represent the different disciplines I interact with in my day to day job. So, there I was in the heart of San Francisco and the energy was insane with anticipation. The room full of aspiring mostly millennial entrepreneurs were there to be inspired by people already successful in the Tech space. Their stories were triumphant and amazing journeys of well-deserved accolades and success but I couldn't help recognizing two things.

1. In many of the stories the successful entrepreneurs had a journey that took them through the corporate world first. Sure, there were a rare few who had built

businesses as college drop-outs but for the most part the vast majority had successful careers in the corporate world before venturing out into the startup world.

2. Secondly, it was mentioned several times throughout the conference that 90% of the aspiring entrepreneurs and their businesses would fail.

As I mixed and mingled with many of the attendees they would tell me about the startup up they were working on and without fail at some point in the conversation they would mention that they were also still working at X corporation. I was struck by how bright, innovative and ambitious they all were and couldn't help thinking that there is such a negative narrative that surrounds working in the corporate world but how ironic it was that the corporate world turns out such amazing wannabe entrepreneurs. I also knew what happened to those 90% when their businesses failed, most of them ended up coming back into the corporate world. The additional irony was that the most successful startups we were hearing from would describe how they grew into what essentially had become a large corporation and tout their wonderful employees who had helped them grow. It was a reminder that every large corporation was once a successful startup.

Every large corporation was once a successful startup

It got me thinking that as a society we have in the recent years skewed towards glorifying entrepreneurship and there is a negative narrative towards working for a corporation. You hear it in the things we say when referring to working 9-5 as:

- The Rat Race

- Working for the man
- Cube monkeys
- Corporate zombies
- Soul crushing work

When in fact what is probably more true about working in the corporate world is that it can be great "on the job training" for building your own business if you are inclined to entrepreneurship. Working in the corporate world is often fulfilling someone's entrepreneurial vision and the best employees are those who buy into that vision. Working at a corporation is in fact working at what used to be a successful startup. Society quite often depicts corporations as these soulless places where robotic people go every day to do their monotonous tasks and yet there I was in a room full of amazing passionate people who had problems they were seeking to solve. I couldn't reconcile the two, my most optimistic self instead posits that the most successful of them would use their corporate skills to go on and build new corporations and to do that they would need great employees who crush it at the corporate game. My hypothesis was that for the most part it was those who were successful corporate employees who then went on to become successful corporation builders.

And yet there was that stat…

90% of startups fail.

I wondered, what if instead of pushing people to become entrepreneurs first we enabled professionals to be better intrapreneurs would we have more successful entrepreneurs? Would we reduce the number of failures? Is 10% the best we can do? I do not know the answer but I believe we must change the negative narrative around working for a corporation and perhaps find a new role for the corporation.

Doing Time

Here's an extreme example of someone who comes off as the antithesis of corporate but in fact is probably a great example of someone who was an exemplary corporate employee. Gary Vaynerchuk is one of my favorite entrepreneurs. If you follow his journey as he tells it goes a little something like this:

> *In his early years as a teen he had several hustles showing early entrepreneurial aptitude. Then as a young adult he joined his father's business and added innovative new ideas that grew the business significantly. In later adult years GaryVee as he is fondly known struck out on his own and became a highly successful tech investor and entrepreneur.*
>
> *As I would tell it I would reframe it saying that in his young adult years he joined a corporation his father was running where he was one of the best intrapreneurial employees implementing innovative ideas that grew the business significantly. He worked there for 13 years before he decided in his mid 30's to branch out. Building on what he had learned working for the man he became the man and is building several successful corporations.*

Another more traditional example would be Oprah Winfrey if you follow her journey as it has been told it goes like this:

> *As an honor student Oprah showed an aptitude for public speaking winning prizes for oratory and dramatic recitation. Because of winning Miss Black Tennessee beauty pageant she was offered on-air job at WVOL Radio where she worked during college. She left college to work at WJZ-TV news as a co-anchor. While there she also co-hosted her first talk show People are Talking. She was then invited to host a show in Chicago WLS-TV where she turned the ½ hour AM morning into a hit show. The show was then expanded to 1 hour and was renamed The Oprah Winfrey show. A year later the show was broadcast nationally and became the top syndicated talk show in the country. In later Adult years after having won numerous awards and accolades and branching out into acting and film she struck out on her own and*

became an entrepreneur starting Harpo Productions which acquired ownership and production responsibilities for The Oprah Winfrey Show becoming the 1st woman to do so and then expanded her business into film production, magazine publishing and the internet.

Her journey to entrepreneurship as I would tell it would point out the journey of "learning the ropes" in the corporate world as follows. Oprah's entertainment career began when she started working at the company WVOL radio after winning Miss Black Tennessee. She dropped college when a job offer to work at another company WJZ-TV news came up moving up to the role as a co-anchor. While there her role expanded to include co-hosting her first talk show "People are Talking". She was then recruited by WLS-TV in Chicago where she moved up to the mornings and she turned the ½ hour AM morning into a hit show. She innovated by changing the format to 1 hour and re-branded the talk show The Oprah Winfrey show. She grew the audience and expanded the footprint a year later nationally and it became the top syndicated talk show in the country. After having won numerous awards and accolades and branching out into acting and film she struck out on her own and became an entrepreneur by starting Harpo Productions which acquired ownership and production responsibilities for The Oprah Winfrey Show becoming the 1st woman to do so and then expanded her corporation into film production, magazine publishing and the internet.

Another example of this is Howard Shultz the former Chairman and CEO of Starbucks as others would tell it.

Howard Shultz grew up in the Bayview projects in Brooklyn, New York. In high school, he was good at sports and received a scholarship to Northern Michigan University where he got his BA in communications. While working for appliance manufacturer Hammarplast Howard noticed a coffee company in Seattle Starbucks was selling a lot of coffee machines and decided to visit the company. After tasting their coffee and learning more about their business Howard decided to join the company. Following a tradeshow trip to Milan where he encountered the idea of coffee shops or the Italian Cafe he wanted to bring the idea back to the US. His bosses at Starbucks were not convinced that it was a good idea. Howard left the company to start his own coffee shop called Il Giornale. His coffee shops were so successful he eventually could buy the Starbucks business and the rest is history.

As I would tell it: with more nuance to the significance of his corporate experience. After graduating Howard was accepted into the sales

11

training program at Xerox where he got experience pitching word processors and cold calling potential customers. He worked there for 3 years gaining experience as a salesman. He then went to work at Hammarplast which was owned by the Swedish company Perstorp where he worked up the ranks to become VP and General Manager running a sales team. The company sold coffee machines and grinders and Howard noticed a coffee company in Seattle Starbucks was selling a lot of these machines and decided to visit the company. After tasting their coffee and learning more about their business Howard fell in love with the company and begged for a year for them to hire him. They eventually agreed and he took a pay cut more than half his pay at Hammarplast and joined Starbucks as their Marketing Director. The next year the company sent him to a tradeshow in Milan where he encountered the idea of coffee shops or the Italian Cafe he wanted to bring the idea back to the US. His bosses at Starbucks were not convinced that it was a good idea. Howard spent 2 years working at Starbucks while he thought about the Coffee House concept. In 1985 he pitched the idea of a network of coffee Houses to the Starbucks CEO. His boss rejected the proposal as his partners believed that coffee was meant to be made and drunk at home. Howard left the company to become an entrepreneur and start his own coffee shop called Il Giornale. His former Starbucks bosses invested in him by giving him part of the startup funding. His coffee shops were so successful he eventually could buy the Starbucks retail business from his old boss. He has since expanded Starbucks into a successful global brand.

You get the idea...much like we like to think companies are overnight successes we also like to think of founders as these magical geniuses who had no corporate life before their entrepreneurship journey'. Jeff Bezos's another good example. He too worked for "The Man" before he became an entrepreneur.

Jeff Bezos graduated Summa Cum Laude from Princeton University and went to work on Wall street. He worked on building a network for trading internationally at the startup Fitel where he rose from debugging code to head of development and then Director of Customer Service. 2 years later because the startup wasn't doing well Jeff sought a more stable job at Bankers Trust where he took the position of Product Manager for 2 years. Then he went to work at D. E. Shaw & Co where he rose to the rank of VP in four years. In 1994 Bezos left his career in finance to start Amazon.com. Bezos was one of the first investors in Google in 1998 and Bezos Expeditions has since then invested in many successful startups like Airbnb, Basecamp, Business

Insider, Workday and Zocdoc to name a few. In 2000 Bezos founded Blue Origin a human space flight company. In 2013 Jeff Bezos acquired The Washington Post.

As you can see even Bezos spent time in the corporate world rounding out his skill set in various roles including product development and customer service. He had operational experience before he ventured into entrepreneurship and it has served him well.

Reverse Engineering Corporate Success

Jay-z the hip-hop artist turned multi-millionaire businessman is a nuanced non-traditional example of an entrepreneur who leverages time within a corporation in a unique way that is also worthy of consideration. Jay-z grew up in the Marcy Projects in Brooklyn, NY where he transitioned from selling drugs in the streets to the music business. He got his start independently through his own label Roc-a-fella Records. Most people who follow Hip Hop music are familiar with his story and the subsequent diversification into other multi-million dollar businesses including Fashion, Restaurants, Alcohol, Sports management and Music technology. So, what is the connection to intrapreneurship? I like to think of Jay-z as a master at reverse engineering corporate success. Jay-z appears to have a blueprint and a modus operandi where he will:

- Step 1: Work within a corporation or partner for a short period of time 1 to 3 years
- Step 2: Learn the inner workings of the core industry and business
- Step 3: Go out on his own and improve on the product or model and dominate.

What you will notice is that whether the opportunities present themselves organically or he actively seeks them out directly he is never a passive participant. He seeks to:

- Maximize the learning even if it means getting certified or putting skin in the game with investment.
- Have a short timeframe
- Understand the strengths and weaknesses of the industry
- Reverse engineer the business model and look to see how he can use what he brings to the equation to improve or disrupt the status quo.

What appears to be hallmarks of his approach in retrospect is passion, perspective, patience and a plan. He focuses on corporations with products that he is genuinely passionate about. He has a perspective that is long-term and involves big-picture thinking about how everything ties together. He then executes a plan that involves being a student for a period. And this all involves having a discipline of patience.

Take a look at some of what I like to call "corporate infiltration" aka #crushingcorporate that Jay-z has done over the course of his professional journey. What you should consider taking away from Jay-z's story is to think of your career as a joint venture with the corporation where you are bringing your skills to the table and the company is bringing resources, learning opportunities and channels to the table for a period of time that you both have the ability to set. But when you leave you are in a much more enriched position figuratively and literally. It is important not to focus on the "what" but the "how" and see how you might translate "his how" to your journey:

1. Music Business:
    a. Passion – Music is his passion but when offered a deal with Def Jam he instead negotiated a deal where they distributed his independent label Roc-a-fella's music.

b. Perspective – amid many changes in the music business that would go on to transform the landscape forever, he goes "corporate" and becomes the President and CEO of Def Jam Records.

c. Patience – Jay-z worked for Universal the behemoth parent corporate company of Def Jam for 3 years, no doubt taking everything in.

d. Plan – Jay-z left the corporation in 2007 but not before he had secured full rights to his masters. Then the 1st thing he did 4 months after his departure from his corporate gig is sign a landmark $150 million dollar 360 deal with Live Nation the 3rd of its kind at the time. It turns out that for anyone who had studied where the music business was going it was the perfect deal to sustain growth in music while others would struggle.

2. Fashion Business:

a. Passion – in 1999 still independent Jay-z started Roca wear urban clothing line with partners. In 2003 he signed a landmark deal with Reebok designing his own shoe that is credited with changing the sneaker industry forever. 2003 was the same year he went "corporate". 2003 is also the year he took over the artistic direction and full charge of Rocawear changing the style away from jerseys and sweats to a more upscale look that sold better.

b. Perspective – in 2007 the same year he left corporate he sold Rocawear for $204 million dollars retaining a stake.

      c.   Patience – He spends 3 years in the corporate world and the year he leaves he signs 2 monster business deals.

      d.   Plan – Roc Nation the company that was funded with the proceeds of the Roc-a-fella sale + Live Nation deal + Rocawear sale now has the music portfolio that includes Rihanna, the technology Powermat a cell-phone-charging device made with Duracell, equity in the Barclays Center real estate projects. movie production e.g. The Great Gatsby, Musical theatre e.g. Fela!, Restaurants the 40/40 Club, The Spotted Pig and The Billionaire Boy's Club.

3.   Alcohol Business:

      a.   Passion – It's well known that rappers tout various products in their videos. Once upon a time Jay-z was a fan of the champagne Cristal until in 2006 the CEO of the prestigious Champagne made some negative comments about the association of his brand with rappers. So, Jay-z and his industry peers boycotted the brand.

      b.   Perspective – Jay-z had a point of view that Cristal was benefitting financially from the mentions it used to get in rapper videos. In 2006 the same year as the boycott - the brand of champagne Armand De Brignac "Ace of Spades" showed up in Jay-z's video "Show me what you got". It turns out that that same year Jay-z invested in the French company that makes Ace of Spades, Chattier.

    c.   Patience – 8 years later the Ace of Spades became one of the most expensive Champagnes in the world and highly awarded #1 numerous times. After 8 years of learning and execution Jay-z acquired the company outright.

    d.   Plan – Once again Jay-z partners with a corporate entity and puts his own brand of expertise, marketing and equity of his personal brand to launch into a new industry. His portfolio now includes the premium Cognac D'usse.

4.   Sports Business:

    a.   Passion – In that epic year 2003 Jay-z hears that the New Jersey Nets are up for sale and the buyer wants to take them to Brooklyn his hometown borough. Developer Bruce Ratner connects with Jay-z and he decides to invest in the team that would become the Brooklyn Nets.

    b.   Perspective – He uses the small stake essentially as a marketing expense that pays for itself. The advertising contract for the Brooklyn Nets was awarded to Translation a marketing agency Jay-z co-owns. He put one of his Sports Bars 40/40 club in the Barclays Center. It is during this period that he signs a deal with CAA and quietly becomes a certified Sports agent. He launches his album "Magna Carta" with a 3 minute ad during the NBA play offs. The release was certified platinum before it even hit the stores because Samsung had bought 1 million copies to giveaway to new subscribers. In the Samsung/Jayz commercial in which he is wearing Brooklyn Nets hat, there is reference to re-writing the rules which some thought was referring only to the music industry but we would soon come to find that he was also referring to what he was about to do in Sports.

c. Patience – 1st learned of the Nets deal in 2003, the deal owner changes in 2008, the project broke ground in 2010. In the summer of 2012 the Brooklyn Nets moved into the Barclays Center.

d. Plan – All this time that Jay-z has been given a peek under covers as an owner of a team he once again flips the script and announces that he is starting his own Sports Agency. He severs his deal with CAA having learned from one of the top agencies in the world. And it is speculated he gives up his stake in the team and has proceeded to stir yet another industry with marquee player signings. No doubt using the learnings as an owner and from his corporate partnership with CAA.

I wanted to dissect Jay-z's Modus Operandi in longer form to give you a sense of another less traditional way you can work within or with corporations to maximize your learning for business success. 2003 when Jay-z went "corporate" was an epic year were he makes many changes and in 2007 when he leaves the corporate world you see him execute on major deals that changed the trajectory of his many businesses. To see if you can detect his blueprint read up on his relationship with Audemars Piguet and Hublots. Jay-z is a #crushingcorporate beast.

(Rice, 2013) (Kafka, 2008) (Welty, 2016) (Greenburg, 2014)

Clearly there must be something to be said for "working for the man" whether you are Gary Vaynerchuk, Oprah, Jeff Bezos or Jay-z. It can be a stepping stone to building great companies and great companies are only great with great employees so why not focus on crushing corporate?

Bringing in the Corporate Guns into a Startup

There is also something obscene about amount of money that is behind the failures that sometimes get glorified. Companies lose millions, investors lose millions and hundreds or thousands of lives are impacted largely due to entrepreneurs who failed. What if instead of denigrating corporations we saw them as a feeder system for driving entrepreneurial innovation. What if our corporations had a mandate to groom entrepreneurs what would the financial and social impact be?

Late 2016 there was an article in Fortune Magazine written by Erin Griffith titled "The Ugly, Unethical Underside of Silicon Valley" Ouch! In it Erin lists the millions lost by numerous failures. She also talks about the fudged numbers, exaggerated traction, compliance and legal regulation ignoring that goes on and in time leads to the inevitable demise of what once seemed ingenious, unstoppable companies. But what I found most interesting was the bubbling worry you read from the VC's she interviewed.

She write's…

> *Some founders grow into talented CEOs. Most don't. That's an inevitable by-product of Silicon Valley culture, where everybody fetishizes engineers, designers, and inventors while managers get little respect. "We have an epidemic of bad management," says Phil Libin, a partner at venture firm General Catalyst. "And that makes [bad] behavior more likely, because people are young, inexperienced, and they haven't seen the patterns before."*
>
> *So, inexperienced people are handed giant piles of money and told to flout traditions, break rules, and employ magical thinking. What could*

19

possibly go wrong? "We hope that entrepreneurs bend the rules but don't break them," McClure says. "You know the saying 'There's a fine line between genius and insanity'? There's probably a fine line between entrepreneurship and criminality." (Griffith, 2016)

What about the startups that do make it? How are they ensuring they grow healthy companies? It feels dishonest to assume that the most successful entrepreneurs use nothing of the skills they learned in corporations to drive the growth of their businesses I know that even if they themselves never worked in a corporation they almost always have advisors or bring on a team of people who have worked in corporations to run the company and drive growth. It is a bit misleading that we think less of the corporate path when it is in fact those who have excelled within corporations who can help turn a startup into a successful corporation. Two examples where wannabe entrepreneurs may be misled into discounting corporate experience are Google and Facebook.

With Google, there are a multitude of reasons why they were a successful startup that has become a massive corporation. Though the founders Larry Page and Sergey Brin will forever be the faces and forces of Google, it is undeniable that they owe some of their success to the fact that they brought in a professional manager in Eric Schmidt. He joined when they were about 200 employees and before they went public his mandate included **"building the corporate infrastructure needed to maintain Google's rapid growth as a company and on ensuring that quality remains high while the product development cycle times are kept to a minimum."** So, who was this guy that the founders brought in to drive the startup's growth stage? Eric Schmidt had worked for the following corporations:

- Bell Labs
- Zilog

- Xerox
- Stanford School of Business
- Sun Microsystems
- Novell

Wouldn't you agree that Eric Schmidt had crushed corporate before he came in to help the startup Google? And you can bet that in setting up the "infrastructure" that the founders had asked him to do he brought in a whole bunch of corporate crushers.

At Facebook, too there are a multitude of reasons why it has become a successful corporation but you would be remiss in not considering the recruitment Sheryl Sandberg as COO as a significant milestone in driving Facebook's dominance. Sheryl Sandberg's early career reads like a mish mash of institutional corporate work:

- McKinsey & Company
- US Treasury Department
- Google

Sheryl spent 7 years at Google where she was their VP of Global Online Sales and Operations She was responsible for online sales of Google's advertising and publishing products as well as for sales operations of Google's consumer products and Google Book Search. Facebook hired her January 2008 before they ever had figured out monetization. Mid-year they had decided on advertising and by 2010 they had become profitable. And the rest is history, while Mark Zuckerberg undoubtedly gets the accolades for steering a formidable corporation to dominance we should be clear about the role of those who are crushing corporate like Sheryl Sandberg.

Evidently the recruitment of excellent operators is a factor for successful entrepreneurs. Could it be that crushing corporate is key to successful entrepreneurship? It should also be noted that Mark Zuckerberg is said to have been mentored by a corporate man 39 years his senior Don Graham. In 2007 Mark emailed Don Graham who was then the CEO of The Washington Post and said, "I'm a CEO now and would like to shadow you and see what you do" He is reported to have spent days shadowing Don learning how to be a CEO and has been mentored by him as Don has sat on the Facebook board passing on that corporate knowhow.

Corporate Badge of Credibility

Isn't it ironic that when entrepreneurs seek funding from VC's what is often drilled into them is that VC's invest in teams and not just the idea. They look at the team and when you unpack what they are looking for you'll hear them say things like domain expertise, management and that the team has worked together before blah blah blah. When you look at look the bios of the teams in their pitch decks quite often you see them showcasing their corporate experience. For example, you'll see "Former Microsoftie" or Microsoft alumni in the Bios. Even the press when they write about the startups will favorably highlight the fact that the founder formerly worked at corporation XYZ. Why is it that employees are looked down on when they work at a company like Microsoft but when they are seeking investment or written about in the press their corporate experience is given value? Why do we value teams with corporate experience when it counts? Why is corporate experience valued when you leave the company but looked at as "selling out" or being a "corporate stooge" when you are at the company? Why hate the company when you are in it but use the tenure there to show credibility and get investment?

Could it be that one of the key's to getting investor confidence or to garner the initial attention of the press for your entrepreneurial endeavors is to be able to point to crushing corporate?

Getting back to the conference... the energy was palpable; the conversations were flowing and ideas were being shared and I was reminded of the times I had felt that same energy and excitement while working at a corporation for example:

The time when I was working for a $500 Million corporate retailer in the early 90's and my team and I convinced the president to start posting the in-store flyer on our website. We were one of the first retailers to do so in Canada. It wasn't the simple act of posting the flier that got me excited but it was the possibility it represented at the dawn of ecommerce.

The time I was working for a unicorn ecommerce site that had now become a huge corporation and my team and I worked with a partner to develop a technology hack that preceded what has now become behavioral targeting. The partner company ultimately got acquired by Google and the unicorn I was working at the time is now a massive corporation eBay.

The time I was working for a monster technology company that had never done any social media marketing or programmatic advertising and our team changed the way they went to market in a few areas including how their sellers drove revenue.

Ideas Born or Given Life in The Corporate World

What becomes clear is that in a lot of those cases it was me as a corporate worker driving the adoption of the developments of entrepreneurs and their innovations. Isn't that interesting? Look at some of the biggest unicorns of our time where would they be if it wasn't for the lowly corporate worker driving adoption of their innovations and isn't it interesting that the corporations themselves are quite often the place where the idea itself is born which is why you often see entrepreneurs come out of a corporation and build a product or service that they then sell back to the very corporation or industry they left? Could it be that the corporation is the place where the entrepreneurial minded should not only go to become better operators but that corporations are one of the places where they can find their unicorn idea?

Instead of maligning going to work for a corporation should we be encouraging it? It feels like an old idea because it is an old idea that has become lost in the hype around Millennials and the work style choices they are making. What is getting lost is the notion of "paying your dues" or "learning the ropes" because there is a negative connotation due to the hierarchical perception of rewarding age or tenure vs. rewarding innovative ideas that is implied. But what we fail to discern is that when you say pay your dues or learn the ropes it can also mean crushing corporate which means:

- Learn everything you need to know about how companies work to make yourself a better operator as an entrepreneur.
- Use the time at the corporation to do big things that will drive credibility and justify you highlighting your experience when you seek investment for a venture or join a startup.
- Find ideas at the corporation that could become businesses or services in and of themselves.
- Use your time at corporations to find your potential co-founder, business partner or ultimate customer.

It seems to me that whether you are working towards building your own corporation or helping fulfill someone else's entrepreneurial vision there is honor in the work you are doing. This book is for people who are currently working in a corporation or coming into the workforce and will likely work for a corporation. This is for those people who recognize that somewhere between "Paying your dues" and "Doing only what you love" is a more nuanced truth that could include crushing corporate while you journey to your dream state. The book focuses on sharing some simple truths about working at a corporation. It is a belief in the idea that you can excel while you are working for a corporation by changing your perspective. I suggest a renewed "Corp" positive narrative that sees working at a corporation as:

- A great opportunity to learn and gain business skills
- A place to find ideas and build your innovation muscle
- A way to discover and hone your strengths
- A place to find potential co-founders and business partners
- A way to build credibility and earn respect in your field

The leap from working in Corporation to leading a Corporation

Quite often the first thing entrepreneurs do when they start their side hustles is print themselves up some business cards that say they are the CEO or VP of this and that. When I say leap to leading a corporation I am not talking about magically becoming a CEO with the magic of new business cards. What I am talking about is the fact that one of the things that working in a corporation can do is give you the skills, experience and knowledge to be a successful CEO to an existing corporation. If you examine your motives and conclude that what you want is to be the Boss one day, then you should consider a few facts.

Some of the most successful CEO's of our time are CEO's who worked their way up within a corporation from entry level positions to become the boss. Take the example of Kenneth Chenault the CEO of American Express. He joined American Express in 1981 and 20 years later became the CEO. I know… to my millennial readers 20 years is going to feel like a lifetime and indeed it is a lifetime. However, it also takes a lifetime to build a sustainable startup into a successful corporation. And when Kenneth Chenault became CEO he took over leading a company that was 166 years old. I don't know about you but that feels like a ton of accountability and the skill level to be able to maintain a global organization of that magnitude is nothing to sniff at. When he got his first set of business cards that said CEO on them they came with an employee organization that numbered in the thousands and a customer base that numbered in the millions. Let's say you can't stand to stay 20 years, you should believe that if you are strategic, that even staying 5 years in a corporation can enable you to amass some valuable skills like Howard Shultz of Starbucks did before you venture out on your own. Howard Shultz was at Starbucks a few years and had General Manager level corporate experience before he ventured out on his own.

Corporation as A CEO Training Ground

You can even be strategic about the corporations you join by choosing those that have a legacy of turning out employees who turn out to be successful CEO's. If you'll recall Howard Shultz came out of Xerox's management training program. It's an old school idea that used to be more talked about than it is these days but should not be overlooked. One company I am amazed by that just has an amazing record for turning out solid operators is the company General Electric GE. This is a company that is 124 years old that is a beast at turning out people who go on to be CEO's of other companies for example James McNerney who worked up the ranks at GE is someone who went on to become the CEO of 3M and then the CEO and Chairman of Boeing.

The other GE example is Robert Nardelli, like McNerney he too rose the ranks at GE and left to become CEO of Home Depot and then Chrysler. 20 years to become the CEO of a 20 or 60-Billion-dollar company! Sounds daunting but if your goal is to be a big boss this is one path that is not talked about enough in my opinion. People leave the corporate world maybe too soon and go off to raise millions of dollars starting their own company only to fail...millions of dollars and hundreds of employees later. Don't get me wrong I am not advocating for staying in corporations for years and years if that is not what you want to do. But what I am advocating for is approaching working at a corporation with a fresh perspective.

- Can you work in a corporation that is aligned to your interests, skills and passion?
- Can you learn what you need to become a highly skilled operator while you are in a corporation?
- If being a boss is what truly interests you, have you counted the costs of becoming the Boss through the corporation vs. striking out on your own?

Look for corporations that have training programs or a legacy of turning out operators. And when you approach the job with this lens you are likely to look for skill building opportunities within the company. If you read the bios of these captains of industry you will see that they worked in very different departments as they rose the ranks which gives them a well-rounded set of skills vs. being specialists. As with most things there are no hard and fast rules. My thoughts are centered around how to increase the likelihood of success when you transition to being the boss or into entrepreneurship. For the more nuanced research on this topic you can read this thoughtful article in HBR titled "Are leaders portable?" by Boris Groysberg, Andrew N. McLean and Nitin Nohria. (Boris Groysberg, 2006)

There is another older Ivey study on the topic that concluded that GE was an outlier as a breeding ground for business leaders. The article titled "General Electric: An Outlier In CEO Talent Development" by Derek Lehmberg, W. Glenn Rowe, Roderick E. White, John R. Philips, concluded that *"Firms led by CEOs who were trained at GE will outperform firms led by CEOs who were not; GE's reputation for developing CEO talent is, in fact, well deserved and not mere hype; and GE appears to develop more CEO talent than other noted CEO talent-generating firms."* (Derek Lehmberg, 2009)

Regardless of whether you agree that there is a correlation with being a great CEO driving growth at any company and having worked in a corporation. There is some value from "sitting at the feet" of 100+ year old companies and as you set off to start your fresh new company or as you start within a 10, 15 or 40-year-old company. One of the people credited at building an environment that bred leaders at GE is the legendary Jack Welch. He believed and shared certain tips that I think are things to look for when you start to work at a corporation. Look for a company that believes these things too:

Jack Welch said:

1. **"You rent the people.** Share your best people across the company" What Jack Welch meant is that you have to allow people to move freely and spend time working in different departments. Look for a company that allows you to move if you see a role that interests you. Of course, there are typically some time constraints that allow for minimal disruptions. Most companies want you in a role for at least a year to 18 months. What you are looking for is managers who have an open attitude about career development and encourages good performers to grow beyond their current role.

2. Jack Welch talked about **the 4 E's Energy, Energizer, Edge and Execution**. You want to look for a company where the leaders have energy and enthusiasm and the employees are energized and excited about the company. You want leaders with edge which Mr. Welch defined as being decisive, quick to say yes or no. You want to stay away from leadership that is in the maybe camp or takes long to make decisions. Finally, execution he defined as

delivering results. You want to look for companies that are doing well or in a growth mode.

3. Jack Welch is also famous for saying **"Control your own destiny or somebody else will"** This quote is powerful whether you are a seasoned professional within an organization or new to the workforce. He was basically saying that in a competitive environment that is sometimes filled with uncertainty companies don't have the time to be telling their employees what to do. Employees should take responsibility for their job and get it done. I like to think that it is the difference between taking an active role in planning and mapping your career vs. just floating along waiting for your career to happen to you.

Are Corporations better at Entrepreneurship than Entrepreneurs?

Do you think of yourself as an entrepreneur? Consider that your entrepreneurial skills might be more successfully employed within a startup that lives within a corporation. An article by Chris Zook at Bain and Company titled "When Large Companies Are Better At Entrepreneurship than Startups" concluded that corporations who start new companies average a 1 in 8 chance of creating a large-scale business. So how do entrepreneurs do in comparison? Per, Zook "1 in 500 will grow to 100M and 1 in 17,000 will grow to $500M and sustain a decade of profitable growth".

Compare that to the typical entrepreneur incorporating a start-up. Bain's research concludes that of all new businesses registered in the US, only about 1 in 500 will reach a size of $100

> *million—and a mere 1 in 17,000 will*
> *attain $500 million in size and sustain a*
> *decade of profitable growth. (Zook, 2016)*

I think the 1 in 500 or 1 in 17,000 stats are compelling odds as most people would be happy with a few million dollars. These odds are better than the lotto. My point in looking at these stats is to impress upon entrepreneurs that you can learn valuable skills from a corporation before you make the leap. Or you can have your entrepreneurial thirst quenched while you are working in a corporation. I also think that we would probably improve the success rate of entrepreneurs if more people spent more time working within a corporation #crushingcorporate in any of the number of ways I have mentioned in this introduction.

The rest of this book is focused on basic skills and mindset you need to have to maximize your time in a corporation. I share my experience of 20 years working in big corporation like Microsoft and eBay as well as startups like Points.com and Lavalife. I have distilled my rules of engagement to Crushing Corporate which are centered on the 4 R's.

1. Reputation
2. Reality
3. Risks
4. Rewards

How to read this book.

If you are new to the workforce or already working in a corporation and interested in figuring out how to make working at a corporation work for you. Each chapter has guidance on getting the most out of your time in a corporation nurturing high performance skills. At the end of each chapter there is a section on how the core guidance can be translated to entrepreneurship.

CHAPTER 1

Reputation in The Corporate World

I was going to start this chapter with a lecture on the difference between a job and a career and give you all the cliché statements I could find about jobs being the thing you do to get money short term vs. the career being the nobler thing you do long-term to fulfill a life-long ambition. I decided against that approach because after 30 years of working,10 years at various "jobs" and 20 years on my life-long career have taught me that to make a distinction between the two is a mistake. If I could put every job I have ever had on my resume I would because each of the jobs from the lowliest corn detasseling job I had when I was 15 to directing marketing at Microsoft have taught me something. With each job, I took away something about myself that has shaped my approach to work. And whether it has been the dead-end retail job I had in my teens or the cool job at a startup, every job has been the building block of a work ethic and ultimately a lifelong reputation. The truth is whether it is a job or a career YOU are the common denominator and if you are looking to excel in your job or career the keys to success are the same.

The truth is whether it is a job or a career
YOU are the common denominator and if
you are looking to excel in your job or
career the keys to success are the same.

Once you start getting paid, look at each job as an opportunity to get a good recommendation or a bad one. It's that simple. If your boss or colleagues were asked "Would you recommend hiring [Insert Your Name Here]?" would the answer be yes or no?

Word of mouth is still the single most powerful way to get a job or promotion and so it is very important that you remember that whatever you are doing now is setting the stage for the next thing you are going to do.

Whatever you are doing now is setting the
stage for the next thing you are going to
do.

The people you work with and your boss are all able to recommend you or dissuade someone from giving you your next role, position or job. Quite often I have seen people treat the work they are doing now as a "pit stop" or "temporary detour" on the way to the ultimate job and in doing that they bring a sub-par work ethic or wear their contempt for their current position quite visibly so that their co-workers and employer can see it in the work they do. Experience has shown me that this is a mistake. You must do good work regardless of the type of job you are doing because what you are doing is building a reputation.

Your reputation is the single most important asset you have as you start to work and gain experience.

Your reputation is the single most important asset you have as you start to work and gain experience

---

I have heard reputation defined as "The widespread belief that someone has a particular habit or characteristic" So when someone is asked "Would you recommend hiring [Insert Your Name Here]?" they are essentially asking not only about your skills and aptitude but also your work ethic and attitude.

Your reputation is the single thing that can make or break your career and ensuring that you are someone people would recommend is the guiding principle to ensuring you crush it in the corporate world. But let's be very clear, having a good reputation is not just about being a "nice" person. It is not about being a person who is a "kiss ass" or who lets people walk all over them. The nuance you must understand about human behavior is that people only recommend people who reflect well on themselves. Your reputation is what ensures people are eager to recommend you and a positive reference usually reflects not only the respect they have for you but that you will reflect well on them.

How do you build a good reputation?

I am sure that there are probably hundreds of tips and tricks I could give you to ensuring you have a good reputation but here are 3 that will ensure you rarely go wrong.

- **Tip #1 Let your work speak.** When you enter the workforce, you will realize that there are many people who talk a good game but are not really doing any work. They might be the people who are loudest in meetings or quick to critique people's ideas or they might be the people always talking about how busy they are or that they have so much work to do. This behavior is okay if it is accompanied by results or actual work that it is clear the person delivered or directed themselves. Either way do not lead with "talk", lead with "doing".

do not lead with "talk", lead with "doing"

- It is the doing and the results that carry the most weight in building your reputation. Over time you will realize that you do not have to do too much talking. Your work can do the talking for you. Lead with delivering results and what you will find is that the quality of your work is what gives you permission to talk the loudest or critique or suggest ideas and have others listen to you.
- **Tip #2 Speak for your work.** When I say speak for your work it might seem like a contradiction to the tip #1 but the nuance is that this is about clarity and ownership. You will notice in the workforce that people will be quick to take credit for good work. Make sure that before you begin a task or project that you and your team mates have a clear understanding ahead of the task completion, who is responsible for doing the task. This means you must take ownership ahead of time for tasks regardless of knowing if you will be successful or fail.

Take ownership ahead of time for tasks regardless of knowing if you will be successful or fail.

- The reality is that people don't respect you because you succeed, over time you will find that people respect those who take ownership regardless of what the results will be. In doing so you will minimize those who seek to take credit for your good work at the end because everyone will know who did the hard work. I know this to be true because there are many respected people who have failed many times throughout their careers but they owned it. Speak for your work...whether you succeed or fail ownership is key to a good reputation.

- **Tip #3 Add value when you speak**. When I say speak in this case I am talking about communication. In the workforce communication is one of the key mechanisms of how work gets done whether it is on the floor talking to your team mates, in meetings, via email, text or conference calls...what comes out of your mouth or how you share your thoughts is an opportunity to add value or not.

What comes out of your mouth or how you share your thoughts is an opportunity to add value or not.

- You want to make sure that your ratio skews more often to adding value. How you communicate is another

35

building block to building your reputation. This one is a hard one to truly internalize until you have made many mistakes. There will be many times you say things and communicate in ways that damage your relationships with people and there are many tools out there to help you build the skills to be an effective communicator. In general, if you equate "adding value" to win/win you will positively impact your reputation. Win/win means that you communicate in a way that ensures that are no losers in your interactions. There is an art in the working world to adding value when you speak by ensuring you get what you need out of an interaction and the other person does too. A win/win approach is not always possible 100% of the time but leaving people with the genuine perception that this was your goal goes a long way to building a solid reputation.

Here are some practical scenarios and how you might apply these 3 tips:

What if I am unemployed how do I build or show my reputation?

Let your work speak - In the digital world we are living in today regardless of your profession or your level of experience you should:

- Own your own domain name and have a digital representation of your work experience in the form of your resume or portfolio including references or testimonials from team mates or employers.
- Have an updated Linkedin profile with recommendations from team mates and employers for each job you have had. Ensure you are connecting with everyone you engage with over the course of your career. Quite often after you have been working in an area it is very likely

that 6 degrees of separation comes into play and there is some connection between you and your potential client or employer.

- Have at least 2 people who can provide as references for potential employers or clients to speak to about you and your work ethic.
- Get reviewed, connected, rated, scored, liked etc. whatever is relevant to your field.

Speak for your work

- On your website and on your Linkedin profile have data points or information that speaks to the results or impact of your work.
- On your website or Linkedin profile show screen shots, images, videos, articles etc. anything that you had a hand in planning, creating, developing, executing or selling.

Add value when you speak

- On your website and elsewhere online share your philosophy or approach to your work.
- If you have the inclination to blogging or vlogging about your field this can be a way to stand out or position yourself as a subject matter expert.

What if I am employed and I want to improve my reputation within my company?

Let your work speak - Do good work. Guard your reputation by being careful to ensure that you are NEVER seen as a slacker. The way you ensure you do good work every day is by adhering to a few rules.

- Make sure you are always clear on what you are being asked to deliver. If you are not clear, ask as soon as possible. Do not wait until it is too late.

- Be clear on when you are expected to deliver by getting precise timing no matter how big or small the task or project is.
- Set expectations right away on what you know you can and cannot do. NEVER pretend or just fake it. If you do not know how to do something either say so right away or get help or the training you need to deliver.

Speak for your work - Share the results of your work successes and failures.

- Be quick to take ownership when things go wrong and be clear on what the cause and solution is going forward.
- Make sure you know what your objective was so that when it is accomplished you can clearly articulate the impact.
- Strive for clarity and ownership even when you are collaborating with others and this may require using tools like RASCI

   R = Responsible for delivering work

   A = Approver/ to whom R is accountable

   S = Support provides support back up

   C = Consultant engaged to provide guidance

   I = Informed those kept informed

Add value when you speak - be a good team player, engage and communicate in a way that ensures everyone wins and keeps their eye on the prize.

- Remember that you all work for the same company in your interactions.
- Know your audience and understand what they are trying to accomplish.
- Look for common goals
- When asked to do a task look for reasons to say yes vs. reasons to say no

- When evaluating an idea someone else has suggested look for reasons why it could work and how you could make it successful
- Remind yourself that it is mostly not what you say that causes conflict but how you say it.

How do I deal with conflict or someone who seems hostile towards me at the workplace or in business?

Let your work speak - Do good work, stop talking.

- It is important to remember that you are not employed to make friends the best you can work towards is respect and to that end delivering good work goes a long way.
- Respect is gained over time through the work you cannot talk someone into respecting you.
- Quality work removes the need to defend yourself.

Speak for your work - Clarity and ownership in roles and responsibilities

- Seek clarity because quite often conflict arises because of a lack of clarity
- The buck stops with you when you are clear on your responsibilities. It is easy to avoid excuses and blaming others if you have clarity right from the start.
- Remember people respect ownership. Apologizing when you take ownership for mistakes quickly builds trust and respect.

Add value when you speak - Look for the win/win in your interactions

- Look for common goals
- Compromise
- Focus on results to do what is best for the task or project

How do I deal with Politics in the workplace?

I define "Politics in the workplace" as the way people use or perceive the power dynamics and social connections at work. It is important that you are not naive about politics. It is a "thing" and others will use it to propel themselves up the ladder but it is one of those areas where you can waste a lot of time and energy unnecessarily. You can speculate all day about politics in the workplace but I choose to focus on the strategies that I have observed to work in my experience in the context of reputation.

Let your work speak - When it comes to power dynamics and social connections and reputation it is much better to be associated with someone who delivers excellent work vs. someone who is good at the politics of looking good. In this case, you play the long game. Sometimes circumstances may look like they are favoring a sweet-talking slacker but 30 years of experience has shown me that "hot air" cannot be sustained and so if you have to align yourself with others then it is best to hitch your wagon to those whose work speaks for itself.

Speak for your work - The workplace is fraught with people who are not satisfied with their role and responsibilities. They might be frustrated with the lack of clarity and ownership and grumble to you or anyone who will hear them. Or they may understand their role but not be happy with the job for a multitude of reasons valid or not. Unless you are their manager it is important that you give yourself a time limit on the number of times you are willing to engage on the topic without a resolution. There is nothing wrong with hearing out a colleague who is frustrated and providing some empathy. But you should ensure that you are not enabling repeated complaint sessions. This applies to yourself as well. You must have clarity about what you want out of your current role and ownership for the solution if you are unhappy. It is good to raise issues you are having to the people who can directly improve or correct the situation. If the person you are talking to cannot directly impact the situation, then you are essentially wasting your breath. When you speak for your work literally it is also a clear way for you to judge whether you are meddling or minding your own business. **Add value when you speak** - Seek win/win situations. You will know when you are gossiping at work. Basically, gossiping is saying stuff behind someone's back that you would not say to their face. Limit the gossip because there is no value to be gained from it and more to be lost if you earn the reputation as a gossip. More common than gossip amongst professionals is the notion of ranting. We are human...ranting happens when we are stressed and or frustrated. What I have seen be effective amongst people who respect one another is to announce that you are about to rant before you do so. People will give you a short window to get it out and collect yourself. Pick and choose wisely who and when you lose it and have a good rant. Remember you are looking for win/win situations ...letting your frustrations out on a colleague at work is rarely acceptable and often is going to require that you apologize at some point. Even when dealing with politics it is important to stay grounded on preserving your reputation. So, do not get involved with messy situations and steer clear when there is no win/win on both sides.

How do I improve my reputation when I am an introvert?

Let your work speak - Satya Nadella CEO of Microsoft is an introvert, Warren Buffet is introverted but their work speaks for itself. Let quality work speak for you and help you build your reputation.

Speak for your work - When you clearly take ownership for your work you do not need to be extroverted. People will know who to go to and who is on point to deliver.

Add value when you speak - It is sometimes challenging to get a word in when you are surrounded by loud extroverts which is why when you get the opportunity to speak it is important that you have well-rounded, cogent thoughts to share that consider both sides. It is more important to add value when you speak than it is to speak frequently.

When I am a minority in the workplace how do I build my reputation?

Whether you are minority woman or man in your workgroup or a person of color or part of the LGBTQ community you will rarely be able to fix societal biases nor is the burden on you in the workplace. However, you should have your eye's wide open and radar on full alert when you assess whether to work for a company. You want to ask pointed questions in interviews, read about and talk to existing staff about the company culture and look at the leadership mix to see whether it is an environment you would be comfortable working in every day. Once you are in the company what I have seen is that it helps to have a mentor/champion. Having a mentor is good for anyone for a multitude of reasons which I will speak to in a later chapter but for minorities it is especially important because you are already starting at a disadvantage if you are a minority and trying to work your way up. Having a mentor or a champion helps counter balance and catch you up to everyone else. After that the same rules apply:

In summary, your reputation is key to success in the workforce. If you have a good reputation it will be clear how eager present and former team mates and employers are to recommend you and provide a positive reference. You can use the 3 tips as a checklist to ensure you will steadily and consistently build a great reputation.

- Let your work speak
- Speak for your work
- Add value when you speak

Reputation as an Entrepreneur

So how does mastering this behavior impact you when you decide to strike out and become an entrepreneur? There are numerous scenarios where this model of building your reputation will come in handy as you build your startup. Here are a few examples:

Quite often one of the first things you should do is recruit some founding partners or specialists to help you get your business off the ground. If you end up asking former colleagues your reputation will either speak for itself or it won't. Especially if you are asking people to work for sweat equity it is not just the idea that will get them excited. I can't tell you how many great ideas I have heard from people I knew just would not be able to pull it off because of a reputation of various factors that just didn't make them worth the risk. And there are also many people who I have known who when I heard they were striking out on their own I just knew they would be successful one way or another given their reputation.

You will find yourself asking friends, family and strangers for money with no guarantee that they will ever get a return on their money. This is 1000 times harder if you have no track record in any capacity of having shown the capability to build and grow anything. I am not saying it cannot be done. I am saying that it is much harder starting with no social proof. It means that all the other factors that people look for should be almost perfect. It changes the decision tree criteria for people when dealing with you. While some people with a good reputation might be able to get money with just the concept and a business plan. You with zero reputation may be held to much higher qualifying criteria. People will want you to build it, test it, prove it before they even think of giving you a dime.

You will find yourself needing help and access to people and resources. Having a good reputation can get you past the "gate keepers" you will truly come to appreciate the notion of "it's who you know" when you become an entrepreneur. But remember that people are willing to recommend you and open their network if they believe you will not reflect badly on them. To come recommended or be connected to someone who can help you people want to know that you are not going to ruin their reputation. You may find yourself leveraging your old corporate network to get you started.

Finally, and probably the most important factor is that when you start a company your values and ethics become reflected in the company and how you treat your customers. Having a good reputation as an individual is a great starting point for having a good reputation as a company. Infusing the traits in your company ensures that you will build solid customer relationships, vendor and partner relationships, investors relationships and employee relationships.

As an entrepreneur using the win/win model and guarding your reputation is an example of how you translate an excellent reputation you earned crushing corporate.

CHAPTER 2

Reality

The legendary leader Jack Welch talks about how his mother taught him "Reality".

"See the world as it is."

I called this chapter reality because if you want to be successful in the workforce regardless of what type of work you are doing it is helpful for you to be grounded in a few realities.

Here are 10 random things that are simple facts about work and working:

1. Unless you are dependent on others, if you don't work you will not eat. You need to work to earn a living. The more skilled, educated or experienced you are the more likely you are to earn a higher living than your peers.

2. Most jobs require 8 hours each day. It is hard to stick to a job you hate for 8 hours a day and do it well. You are

more likely to find success earning a living doing what you enjoy and are good at. Cliché but #facts.

3. Employers will look at how long you have stayed at your previous role before they consider hiring you so choose the roles you accept wisely because leaving a role in less than a year raises flags about your commitment and resilience.

4. Staying in a role too long also raises flags. If you like a company, you should ensure you are growing within the company and changing roles and responsibilities every two years. You make your mark in a role in year one by having 1 thing you successfully drive. Cement your legacy by optimizing it in year 2 and then move on to the next thing. It is reasonable to work towards getting promoted every 2 years. As you get more senior it might be every 2-5 years but you should ensure that on your resume you can cite growth every few years if you worked at the same company for some time.

5. The best way to get a big upward shift in your salary is to change companies or business groups. Sometimes there are no open positions at your existing company and it may take too long for one to open. When you change companies, you can almost always guarantee a pay increase unless you consciously choose to make a lateral move or take a pay cut.

6. Sometimes it makes sense to take a pay cut with a smaller company or Startup if it means you get a better opportunity to advance your skills and experience or if you think the company is going to grow fast with you benefiting from being an early employee.

7. Companies are made up of people and it is the leadership that shapes the culture. Before you join a company look

at the management and their employees to see if you can see yourself amongst them. Check out the company's social media accounts and see what their customers are saying. Watch interviews of their leadership and study their mission and values to see if you can see yourself working with them. The single most important relationship you have in a company is the one you have with your manager. Managers control how you are perceived and hold the key to your growth within the company. Interview the company instead of thinking you are being interviewed.

8. Being evaluated is a part of what you agree to when you are working for anyone other than yourself. You are not only evaluated on whether you deliver the work but most often what is being evaluated is how you deliver the work. Is it on time, good quality, expected or exceeding results, do your peers like working with you, would they recommend promoting you? Be prepared to be evaluated on a regular basis.

9. The best time to find a job is when you already have a job. Always ensure you have your resume updated and connect with people on Linkedin because you never know where your next opportunity will come from.

10. Being fired or laid off is also a reality of being in the workforce. However, if it happens to you it should be rare that it is a complete surprise. There are usually signs that either you are going to be fired or laid off. In the case of being fired most cases it is based on your performance or sometimes a change in management might result in the new manager bringing in their own people. In the case of being laid off there are usually signals that the business is not doing well or that the business group is

not performing well. Either way do not allow yourself to be caught off-guard always have a game plan.

Ok now that you are grounded in the basics let's get to the nuanced aspects of working.

Self-awareness

Probably the most important thing you can do for your career is to be self-aware which has been defined as "The conscious knowledge of one's own character, feelings, motives and desires" You should check-in with yourself often or as they say, "Know Yourself." In the context of being in the workforce consider the following as we breakdown "Self-awareness":

Character

Your character is your personality or mental and moral qualities that make you the distinctive individual you are. I believe that as you gain more experience and mature your opportunity to become more self-aware increases. I won't attempt to address morality for many reasons but in the context of work I do think looking at your personality is very important. The reason why it is helpful for you to have clarity on your personality is it can provide general guidance on the types of professions and roles that your type of personality is suited for. There are a many personality tests that have been used over the years by organizations to help employees be more self-aware of their innate tendencies, strengths and weaknesses as well as guidance to understand others you work with. One such test is the Myers Briggs test which I first took when I was working at eBay in 2003 and at that time my results were ENTJ I took the test again in 2016 and got the same results ENTJ. I was informed at the time that ENTJ is a very rare combination. Using myself as an example let me share how you use the results of a personality test. This is what they say about the ENTJ personality.

www.my-personality-test.com Results Source: (Copy below is directly from my results):

- Charismatic, natural leaders
- Focused and determined
- Decisive, efficient, and direct
- Great problem solvers and planners

Strengths

ENTJs are natural leaders and are great problem solvers. To an ENTJ, there is no problem that cannot be overcome, and they enjoy nothing more than reaching their goals. Others are naturally drawn to them, and ENTJs have a knack for getting others onboard with their ideas. ENTJs hold themselves and others to a very high standard. They always try to learn from their mistakes, doing their best to avoid making the same mistakes again in the future. ENTJs have the rare ability to visualize the future they desire, and can put it into a plan of action. This is evident in both their personal life and work life. In their personal life,

ENTJs enjoy setting goals for themselves, and are always looking for ways to better themselves. In their work life, ENTJs can visualize where their project or company is headed, and plan to achieve this.

Weaknesses

While ENTJs enjoy leadership roles and solving problems, they often may seem "pushy" when sharing their ideas with others. ENTJs must remind themselves to make others feel heard, even when ENTJs don't agree.

Because ENTJs do not like themselves or others making mistakes, they may become impatient with others who are less competent than themselves. They focus more on efficiency than the needs and feelings of others, which can often be problematic. ENTJs are best fit for leadership roles and may have trouble working as a team—especially if their team members are feeling (F) types. Similarly, ENTJs' desire for efficiency and practicality may lead them to neglect thinking about the bigger picture or complex theories. They may tend to make decisions without considering all the possible options. Others may view them as impatient.

Work Habits

ENTJs are strong communicators and are great for leadership positions in their career. ENTJs are often described as visionaries. ENTJs are easily able to identify a problem, find a solution, and make a detailed plan to achieve this solution. ENTJs have the rare ability to consider both theoretical ideas, as well as the practical implications. ENTJs are usually well-liked by their coworkers and superiors in the workplace. However, they have little patience for others who are less competent than themselves. This can make ENTJs come off as harsh to others—particularly their subordinates. ENTJs must remind themselves to consider the feelings of others. They must try to let others know how appreciated and valued they are – something that ENTJs often forget about in the hustle and bustle of things.

Career Paths

ENTJs have no problem making their career the focal point in their lives, and because of this, are a great fit for careers that are highly-demanding and time-consuming. ENTJs are often well-suited for careers as entrepreneurs, consultants, lawyers, judges, managers, and university professors/administrators. (My-personality-test.com, 2016)

When you take this test or other similar tests it is important that you understand that it is merely guidance. In my experience when my colleagues and I have taken these tests it has been very helpful in validating what we already knew but also provides clarity on why another person is the way they are. It helps in understanding what you value and what others value which provides insights that make collaboration easier. What is most helpful early in your career is that it can also give you enough self-awareness to steer you away from careers and roles you will be unhappy in and towards careers that will leverage your strengths.

How did I use it?

Going into the technology industry made sense for me because I like to be forward thinking and my visionary skills would be appreciated. Being in a place where you must come up with new ideas has made sense for my personality. The field of marketing where there is both art and science appealed to my extroverted and analytical nature. It also made sense why my initial journey in university to become a dancer failed. While I loved to dance, the circumstances were not such that I could become a leader. My skillset and interest were not enough to propel me in that industry.

Feelings

On your journey to "self-awareness" being aware of your feelings can impact how you interact with others. Organizations have started to use practices like NVC which stands for Non-violent Communication. The practice of NVC was developed by Marshall Rosenberg to enable people to express and receive communication with empathy. It may on the surface sound very fluffy and superficial however I have found it to be very powerful with deepening your self-awareness and results in being a much more effective communicator particularly when it comes to dealing with conflict situations. I recommend the book Non-Violent Communication - The Language of Life by Marshall Rosenberg to deepen your learning. (Rosenberg, 2003)

Motives and Desires

As you continue the journey to self-awareness the book by Simon Sinek "Start with Why" focuses on how to do things which inspire you. Find out what motivates others and more important what motivates you. Mr. Sinek created a simple model called "The Golden Circle" which prompts you to ask yourself to find your "Why" His conclusion is that people don't buy "what" you do they buy "why" you do what you do? (Sinek, 2009) In the work-place there will be many times when you will seek to share your ideas and convince others to support you. Being self -aware of why you do what you do will give you the ability to communicate and connect others emotionally getting them to understand and connect with what you believe.

Why the focus on Self-awareness? When you understand yourself and what makes you tick you can get clear on what jobs, companies and cultural environments make sense for you. You want to set yourself up for success and by being true to yourself. Doing this will help you make decisions that will have a higher probability for success. Being self-aware also helps you get clarity on your strengths and weaknesses giving you the confidence to know which jobs you will be successful at and which ones are not for you.

When you know how to assess yourself you also understand how to assess others and can determine which people you will be able to work with easily and what personality types are a challenge. You will not be able to get along with everyone all the time but you can be proactive about how to adjust your workstyle with certain personalities.

Emotional Intelligence

Self-awareness leads to Emotional Intelligence also known as EQ. "Emotional intelligence is your ability to recognize and understand emotions in yourself and others, and your ability to use this awareness to manage your behavior and relationships."

And why is Emotional Intelligence important? It is THE single factor found to be the difference in why people with average IQ's outperform people with higher IQ's 70% of the time. (Goleman, 2012) Many years of research have found that top performers have high emotional intelligence. The challenge with EQ is that it is hard to measure because it is about awareness and mastery of your emotions.

Here are 10 signs of people who are Emotionally Intelligent

1. Rather than saying they are "mad" about something people with EQ are nuanced in articulating what they are feeling and why for example, I am frustrated because of the impact delays will have on the project. I am demotivated because I am not empowered to make decisions. Emotionally intelligent people can articulate their emotions with precision and therefore get to the root cause which usually reveals potential solutions. When you can do this for yourself you can identify problems fast and address them quickly. You are also able to recognize potential problems ahead of time and know how to avoid them.

2. People with EQ are also curious about people. They recognize that nothing gets done alone in the workforce and so they study people and that curiosity is a result of empathy or "giving a damn" "caring". People who care

53

tend to be more thoughtful about what it is going to take for a project or initiative to succeed.

3. People with EQ are always ready for change and they adapt to it easily. In fact, they are rarely surprised by change because they are the one's looking for it and they embrace change when it comes.

4. People with EQ are good at reading people and are good at judging character. They are very socially aware and understand what might be motivating people to behave a certain way. They will be good at motivating people and spotting talent.

5. People with EQ know not to take things personally because they have a strong sense of self. They will not be easy to offend and have a combination of confidence and thick skin that makes them able to navigate a world where the lines between humor and shame may be blurred.

6. People with EQ get enough sleep.

7. People with EQ know when they should say no to requests that will distract them.

8. People with EQ work with what they have and avoid comparing themselves to others.

9. People with EQ understand that failure is to be expected sometimes and when it happens can take lessons from it that will impact future initiatives.

10. People with EQ know how to take a break from work, reset and restore coming back refreshed and revived and able to perform even better.

Daniel Goleman who is the co-director of the Consortium for Research on Emotional Intelligence in Organizations at Rutgers University and Richard E. Boyatzis who is a psychology professor wrote in a recent Harvard Business Review article "Don't shortchange your development as a leader by assuming that EI is about being sweet and chipper, or that EI is perfect if you are – or, even worse, assume that EI can't help you excel in your career" They have shared a framework that the HR nerds can appreciate and that will add value for you to model. In their framework EI has 4 components as follows:

- Self-awareness
- Self-Management
- Social awareness
- Relationship management

In each of these components are competencies that you can choose to work on that will help you mature your Emotional Intelligence as follows:

SELF AWARENESS	SELF MANAGEMENT	SOCIAL AWARENESS	RELATIONSHIP MANAGEMENT
Emotional Self-Awareness	Emotional Self-control	Empathy	Influence
			Coach and Mentor
	Adaptability		Conflict Management
	Achievement Orientation	Organizational Awareness	Teamwork
	Positive Outlook		Inspirational Leadership

(Boyatzis, 2017)

I encourage you to explore each of these areas throughout your corporate journey. There are many models and approaches you can take. Self-awareness is a key aspect of emotional intelligence and having a high EQ enables you to outperform even people who have a higher IQ.

Sphere of Control

The second element to ground you is the notion of understanding your "Sphere of Control". This is important because in the workforce and over the course of your career there are going to be many things to complain about and many decisions made by others that may frustrate you. You can use the Sphere of Control as a tool to prioritize what you should spend your time on and how you should spend it.

There are 3 aspects to be aware of as follows:

- The areas you control
- The areas you can influence
- The areas you have no control or influence over

By process of elimination it makes absolutely no sense to whine and complain repeatedly about areas where you have no control or influence. The keyword here is "repeatedly". There is nothing wrong with sharing your frustration or point of view occasionally but if there is nothing you can do about it directly then you should waste no time on it.

If you can influence an area but do not have direct control over it, you can offer yourself or POV to the team that has direct responsibility. The key thing here is how you offer up your opinion. If it comes as a form of criticism, then it is likely to be reacted to defensively. If it comes as a form of concern or aid it is likely to be reacted to favorably. Most of the time in the work world you are working in teams where you and your colleagues all have influence. Key here is if you are not the person who ultimately makes the final decision you should be prepared without taking it personally for your idea or opinion to be rejected. Know when to pick your battles and remember you have done your part to add value where you can but your core responsibility is the area you directly control. The area you control is where you should put your best effort and most time. This is the area that you will be evaluated on. This is "your lane" within your direct sphere of control. There is a lot to be said for staying in your lane.

Here are the top 5 reasons to focus on the areas you control.

1. Staying in your lane - allows you to become a SME (Subject Matter Expert) in your area. You become the "go to" person that others rely on or send other people to for guidance or suggest consulting on best practices.

2. Staying in your lane - allows you to focus without distraction and with enough time especially if you have clarity on your responsibilities.

3. Staying in your lane - allows you to focus on problems in your area of control and since you are the key decision maker you can decide on solutions that resolve those problem areas.

4. Staying in your lane - allows you to take credit justifiably for improvements that are a result of your work.

5. Staying in your lane - allows you to establish trusted and sustained relationships with your peers and leadership.

Interviewing the Company

It is important that you never put yourself in a position where you are desperate for a job. Therefore, it is better to look for a job when you have one. This gives you the best leverage with your existing company and the new potential company. Either way your perspective should be that you are interviewing the company not the other way around. Is this role, manager and company right for you? Your game plan should be divided into 3 components:

Before the interview

1. Ask and get the names of the person/people you will be interviewing with and look them up on Linkedin, other

social networks and search engines. You want to understand their roles, experience and high level guess of what they care about relevant to their job and how it intersects with the role you are applying for.

2. Review the Job Description and understand the sector your role is focused on then make notes on the top 5 industry or sector trends.

3. Note who the companies top 3 competitors are visit their websites and social accounts to get a sense of how they are positioning themselves relevant to the company you are interviewing with.

4. Visit the company's websites, social accounts and visit review sites to understand what the company says about themselves and what their customers are saying about them.

5. Create a presentation that includes a 5-page visual overview of you can you will forward to them ahead of time. The sections will be as follows:

    a. Me at a glance - personal details, family and interests

    b. Business achievements - key accomplishments,

    c. Career path/ journey - visual journey of former workplaces and roles

    d. Key strengths - core characteristics

    e. 1st 90 days - how you would approach 30, 60 and 90 days on the job

6. Review your resume, dates and timelines and rehearse describing your career history, articulating your interest in the role and company. Also, listen to yourself talking about trends in your industry and profession.

7. Prepare and practice 5 questions you will ask interviewers about the role, the company and what success looks like.

8. Have practiced answers to the most common interview questions as well as the awkward questions like salary requirements, why you are leaving current company etc.

   - What does success look like for the person in this role?
   - What makes you proud to work at X company?
   - How does the company celebrate success?
   - Regardless of titles who in the company has the power to get things done?
   - What has been your favorite moment at the company?

During the interview

1. Relax. Your goal is to communicate your interest in the company, show you understand the role, communicate the skills and experience that you bring to the table. Most importantly you are there to see if the company and manager are right for you.

2. Strike the right balance between being friendly and being reassuringly competent. Remember that people secretly have contempt for over-smiley, over talkative people but they want to be able to see themselves being able to "stand" 8 hours a day with you. So, balance is the key and you want to leave the interviewer feeling you are interested in the opportunity, passionate and knowledgeable about your profession.

3. Watch for non-verbal cues. What do you do with your hands when nervous, expressions on your face.

4. Watch the tone of your voice and speed that you are talking.

5. Dress in business casual regardless of the culture of the place. You just need to show you can "clean up" and it shows that you take the opportunity seriously.

6. Suggest talking them through your personal presentation so that you can control the journey of conversation. Some interviewers will ignore the presentation and prefer to just talk so do not push or insist most will note your diligence and you will have an edge over other candidates.

7. From your research on Linkedin and social accounts you may find that you have connections in common with the person interviewing you. You may have people you both know, former employers in common, schools or interests. Find a way to mention them without sounding like you are a stalker over the course of the interview.

After the interview

1. Send the obligatory thank you note but differentiate yourself by referencing something from your conversation and perhaps adding a relevant piece of research, article or industry trend.

2. Connect with everyone you interviewed with on Linkedin.

3. If you get an offer from the company, you want to make sure you get full market rate or better. Here are a few things to keep in mind:

   a. You want to lead with your excitement about the opportunity when negotiating your salary.

   b. Use sites like Glassdoor and pay scale to get a sense of what the salary is for someone with your years of experience, in your location gets paid. Be aware that there is a salary range and you want to ask for what is fair within that range. Also, talk to your peers in the field and at other companies to get a sense of real salary ranges.

c.   Keep in mind that your grades or school are irrelevant to most hiring managers. So, that is not a strong talking point.

d.   Keep in mind that the average yearly promotions are 2-3% so if their initial offer is within the market range but you would like more you should be asking for salary increases in 3% increments within the range.

e.   Consider the full package including signing bonus, stocks, vacation time, relocation package which are good levers for negotiation. Then also look at the value of the health benefits, transportation, food and fitness perks.

f.   Be quick with your responses but use email to give you enough time to evaluate the offer. If you receive the offer via a phone call, ask to see the offer in writing via email to have time to evaluate it.

4.   If you have another offer from another company be honest about the amount do not over inflate the numbers as most recruiters are aware of the range in the industry.

5.   If you are asked about your previous salary be truthful. If you were being under-paid, make it clear that you know this and are looking to be within the market range. Be data driven and include links to the numbers that make sense for your experience and location.

6. In your research make sure you account for the cost of living if you have to move to a new city and include that in the negotiation.

7. If you have unvested stocks you are leaving in your current role include the value of them in your negotiations as an incremental bonus, ask.

8. Negotiate your start date and notify them of any vacation that has already been booked so they are aware.

9. It is also now that you should mention any special arrangements you have that may affect your day to day like if you must pick up kids from daycare at a specific time. Or if you need to work from home on a specific day. It is important to be upfront before you join the company to ensure that you set expectations and to see if theirs is a culture that fits your lifestyle.

10. There will be cases where you are willing to take a pay cut because of the opportunity or because it is a smaller company. In this case, you want to negotiate either a higher title so that next time you step back into the market you can command a higher salary. You can also ask for more stock in lieu of the salary you are losing.

11. Throughout the process lead with positive energy and excitement.

Education vs. Experience

The last aspect of reality I want to address is the role of education vs. experience in career progress and high performance. There is nothing I can tell you that is set in stone because everyone is different and there are things that are specific to certain professions. Obviously for careers that require specific certification, licenses, degrees to legally work in the field there is no getting around it. What I am talking about is fields where there are many paths to progressing up the career ladder or reaching the pinnacle of success in a profession.

Here are some generalizations to keep in mind just as guidance:

You should NEVER let your lack of formal or institutional education in a field stop you from pursuing a career in that field. There are many informal ways to get into a field and resources outside of a formal education that can get you to the same level of knowledge as someone who has learned through an institution.

In all my years of working I have NEVER hired anyone solely based on their education in fact outside of internship or entry level positions I rarely take where a person went to school into consideration in a decision to hire someone.

In looking back at the many people, I have hired over the years very few have had a degree related to the field I was hiring for.

In all cases where I have been directly responsible for hiring someone years of experience has superseded the prestige or the formality of their education.

I have never required an MBA but have hired MBA's or have worked with MBA's but have rarely found instances where having an MBA has been a factor to high performance.

When it comes to education vs. experience I have found that folks who learned on the job and continue to do so throughout their career tend to be high performers particularly if they always maintain an interest in innovations in their discipline.

Imposter Syndrome

Clinical psychologists Pauline Clance and Suzzane Imes first coined the term "Imposter Syndrome" in 1978 describing when high achieving people sometimes feel like they are not smart, skilled or creative. It has been written that people who are experiencing Imposter Syndrome describe a feeling of phoniness and they have a hard time internalizing their accomplishments and have a persistent fear of being exposed as a fraud. (Imposter Phenomenon, 1978)

At some point or even several times in your career you will encounter this feeling. Fears and doubts when you are about to propose something innovative or try something new or do something outside your comfort zone. You may experience a voice that asks you:

- Who do you think you are to try and do this?
- What makes you think you are even qualified to do or try this?
- How can you think you are good enough?

You may even be paralyzed into doing nothing because you are haunted by the fear of being an imposter. Well the 1st thing you need to know is that this feeling has a name and you are not the only high achieving person to feel this way. I love this article on the Imposter Syndrome that Carl Richards wrote about it in the NY times where he talks about Maya Angelou feeling like a fraud even after having written 11 books. And Presidents sitting in the Oval office thinking to themselves "I hope nobody finds out I'm in here" Seth Godin who has written many best sellers writing in his book "Icarius Deception" that he still feels like a fraud. (Richards, 2015) The core insight I took away from this article is the notion that when something comes easy to us we tend to discount its value. But it is irrational because if we have spent time practicing a skill or working a field it stands to reason that is should look like it comes naturally to us. Refined experience and talent looks natural but shouldn't be valued less.

The fears and doubts can paralyze you and stop you from taking risks and doing big things. Here are some tips to dealing with Imposter Syndrome and making sure you don't sabotage yourself.

- Just do you - Life is much easier when you forget about competing with others or trying to be perfect. Just focus on being the best version of yourself. The phrase "Bring your A game" is appropriate with the key word being "your".

- Luck is for the birds - Do not make the mistake of attributing your milestones solely to luck. Acknowledge your own hard work. We spend a lot of time focused on the things we haven't done but when you are experiencing doubt it can help for you to acknowledge how far you have come and celebrating the hard work it took to get you to this moment.
- Embrace the feeling - You have two choices You can choose to know or to never fail.
- Fake it till you make it - There are many people who have studied successful people and one of the things that they do is they act confident even when they don't feel confident.
- Be your own hype man - High performance coaches will sometimes refer to this as "Self-talk" I have for years referred to it as being your own best cheerleader. Talk to yourself and tell yourself what you already know that "You can do this". Be your own Muhammad Ali.

Dr. Valerie Young who is a speaker and expert on Imposter Syndrome writes the following that I found helpful:

"Being bold is not about being right, being perfect, or knowing it all. Rather it is about marshaling resources, information and people. It involves seeing problems as opportunities, occasionally flying by the seat of your pants, and ultimately being willing to fall flat on your face and know you will survive." (Young, 2011)

The reality is that building anything whether it is your career or company takes time and grit. Simon Sinek has an interesting take on why Millennials are struggling in the corporate world which you can hear in a video that went viral. "Simon Sinek on Millennials in the Workplace." While I didn't agree with all his conclusions I do agree with the notion of some millennials not having the patience because of they are used to having instant gratification. Which is why I emphasize the "long game". Many will have more fulfilling careers if they accept that anything worth having takes time and as Sinek says Millennials talk about wanting to have impact like it's the peak of a mountain but ignore the fact that the mountain must be climbed.

Reality as an Entrepreneur

So, we talked about self-awareness, Emotional IQ, sphere of control, interviewing the company, education vs. experience and Imposter syndrome. Having experience with handling each of these areas will prepare you for entrepreneurship. Here are a few ways:

People who are self-aware have likely done the work to accept themselves and focus on their strengths. You can recognize these people because even if they are nervous it's an excited, confident, authentic nervous energy. Not a worried, unsure, petrified energy. As an entrepreneur you will be convincing and persuading people to do things for you and with you. Those who are emotionally intelligent don't just have their book smarts to rely on but they also have an ability to connect with others and understand their motivations and how to align with them. These are the people who can read the room and adjust. They are the people who know when to stop talking and listen. They know when to adjust to an informal chat vs. do a formal presentation. As an entrepreneur self -awareness will make you a better storyteller, better connector and better at how you show up. The other aspect that happens with entrepreneurs is that sometimes they may have to change their idea or "pivot" as it is often referred to. Having the maturity and awareness not to be defined by a certain idea makes it easier to let go and move on to a more successful path.

Sphere of control becomes critical when you are an entrepreneur. You take on many roles and your resources are drastically reduced now that you don't have a big company behind you. You must become hyper focused and minimize the distractions to get stuff done and move on to the next milestone. You cannot be obsessed with what the competition is doing because that is beyond your sphere of control. You can become obsessed with what your customers are doing because that is within your sphere of control. You cannot be paralyzed when you get rejected because you have zero to minimal influence of the decision criteria that investors have. An entrepreneur is measured by the milestones and traction that is within their control.

The practice of interviewing the company will fare you well when you are in a position where you have multiple investors or multiple partners who want to work with you. It is important that you are not coming from a position of desperation that you are thinking long term about the relationships you will be going into with these entities and make choices that will be good for your well-being and the health of your company.

When it comes to education vs. experience there are going to be some areas as an entrepreneur that no book, webinar or MBA class could have prepared you for. You simply just have to go through it. This is quite often true when it comes to how you go to market. This is why the notion of growth hacking is popular amongst startups. Because sometimes you just do not know what is going to happen unless you test it. In the book, Rework by the folks from 37signals they say, "planning is guessing" The point is not so much about not planning... planning is a good discipline but you cannot fall in love with your plans and hypothesis. Having a healthy attitude about education vs. experience will also help you learn to take ideas from all sources. It also applies to looking at the people you hire and learning that good employees may have different backgrounds which when brought together can be powerful.

Imposter syndrome is real when you are just a small team who believe in a single idea. There are going to be many things that happen to cause you to doubt your idea. You will get conflicting advice and you will have many tough days. You will doubt yourself numerous times but having the discernment that comes with embracing and pushing past will only increase your grit which is key to sticking to your goals for the long haul. As you do when you are working within a corporation let the data do the talking rather than your internal subjective doubts.

CHAPTER 3

Risks

The longer you work in your field and the more experience you get over time you will begin to notice a few things. The people who get promoted fastest don't get promoted for doing their job well, they get promoted for doing more than is expected. Essentially, they exceed expectations and are rewarded for doing so. "Doing more" can come in two forms:

1. You can do your job better than anyone else in a similar role. For example, if you are a salesman you can get the highest sales or if you are a marketer you can lead a campaign that gets the highest response rates.

2. You can improve the job process or develop or bring in a new way to do something that impacts your business positively directly.

Again, the key thing you must understand is that you don't get promoted for just doing your job. You can do your job well and still not get promoted because you have been paid the salary you agreed to do the job. Although tenure and length of service is appreciated it alone is not necessarily reason enough to get promoted. It is going over and above what is expected that typically gets you promoted. Demonstrating skillset and executional maturity beyond your current role is what gets you considered for promotion. You will come to know the people who deserve to be promoted and recognize the types of initiatives that deserve acknowledgement. Promotions are because of positive outcomes and significant business impact for example:

- Driving increased sales
- Saving the company money
- Making the company more efficient
- Making more customers happy, loyal advocates
- Increasing the speed
- Reducing mistakes
- Improving outcome rates
- Finding a new revenue channels
- Finding new markets and customer bases
- Enabling new tools, practices or capabilities
- Making teammates better
- Enabling data insights that the business can use

Being a Top Performer

Let us break down the first way to "do more" by doing your job better than anyone else. To be a top performer it requires a combination of a few things for example:

1. Organizational intelligence - knowing how your company works, maximizing all the resources available to you.

2. Clarity on your goals - having a measurable plan on how to achieve your goals

3. Knowledge and adoption of the most modern or best performing tactics that people in your profession are using.

4. Use of data to give you an edge in prioritizing your focus on the biggest opportunities

5. Grit - Top performers tend to have resilience that drives them to push through obstacles that under normal circumstance would stop others.

Breaking down the second way to "do more" by being a problem solver:

There are many examples of ways people put themselves in a position to be promoted but what is common about most cases is that these people tend to be Intrapreneurs.

Intrapreneurship

Intrapreneurship is defined as the act of behaving like an entrepreneur while working within an organization. These are the people who take risks within the context of their job to solve a given problem. These folks either identify a new market opportunity or a new way of doing things outside of their day to day scope of work.

Intrapreneurs deliver value in the following ways:

1. Drive increases in productivity by taking risks to find a better way of doing things.
2. Drive innovation in a company by taking on tasks that increase the capacity.
3. Drive finding ways for companies to move or optimize faster.
4. Intrapreneurs see trends and know where the company needs to go before anyone else.
5. Intrapreneurs up-level the skill set of other employees because they invest in their own skills and bring those learnings to the broader company.

Gifford Pinchot author of the book Intrapreneuring detailed the following commandments:

- Come to work each day willing to be fired.
- Circumvent any orders aimed at stopping your dream

- Do any job needed to make your project work regardless of your job description.
- Find people to help you
- Follow your intuition about the people you choose, and work only with the best.
- Work underground if you can - publicity triggers the corporate immune system.
- Never bet on a race unless you are running in it.
- Remember, it is easier to ask for forgiveness than for permission.
- Be true to your goals, but be realistic about the way to achieve them.
- Honor your sponsors.
- Ask for advice before asking for resources.
- Express gratitude
- Build your team, intrapreneuring is not a solo activity
- Share credit widely
- Keep the best interests of the company and its customers in mind, especially when you must bend the rules or circumvent the bureaucracy.
- Don't ask to be fired; even as you bend the rules and act without permission, use all the political skill you and your sponsors can muster to move the project forward without making waves. (Pinchot, 1986)

Failure

This might be a very generalized statement but it strikes me that you cannot be a top performer by playing it safe, you must take risks. But in taking risks your chances of success are 50/50 so you are likely to have huge failures as well. Therefore, you should have a very grounded perspective on failure to be successful. First I would recommend you read the following article from Harvard

Business Review on <u>"Strategies for learning from Failure"</u> it is the most nuanced and brilliant dissection of failure that I have ever come across by Amy C. Edmondson

You will get tremendous value from reading and re-reading it and internalizing the approaches to designing and learning from failure that apply to your business. I found her last thought to be sobering.

"But most managers I've encountered in my research, teaching, and consulting work are far more sensitive to a different risk—that an understanding response to failures will simply create a lax work environment in which mistakes multiply.

This common worry should be replaced by a new paradigm—one that recognizes the inevitability of failure in today's complex work organizations. Those that catch, correct, and learn from failure before others do will succeed. Those that wallow in the blame game will not." Amy C. Edmondson (Edmonson, 2011)

There is much to learn but I'll share some simple thoughts on failure that in my years of experience have never steered me wrong:

1. Understanding what went wrong is much more valuable and productive than figuring out who is to blame. In trouble-shooting or in doing post mortem's try to take people out of the equation and simply look at steps in the process or steps in the experience. There are some cases where much can be learned if people involved

understand that there will be no negative repercussions for mistakes or unforeseen issues.

2. Conversely there are certain actions in specific industries where not adhering to rules and regulations does deserve severe consequences. But what is key being that the compliance checks are well socialized and widely communicated as standard practice BEFORE anyone takes risks with new initiatives and practices. For example, in certain industries putting customer data at risk is unacceptable and so that is something that should always be checked before a new initiative goes live. In certain industries taking short-cuts on quality or best practices can put human beings in danger of injury or death.

3. I have been fortunate to have worked at companies where the mantra of "Failing Fast" has been internalized and how that typically plays out is designing pilot programs or tests to roll out in phases minimizing scope small enough to get statistically representative results before rolling out more broadly.

4. Having said that do not launch pilots in perfect conditions. Conduct pilots in the real conditions because there is no perfection in the real world. Plan for the lowest common denominator. Design your tests for the worst circumstances e.g. little to no service, old computers or people who are not tech savvy etc. Mimicking real world conditions allows you to surface real world issues.

5. Plan for failure ahead of time and have the potential risks documented when you are proposing an initiative or a risky project this allows you to anticipate failure, set expectations and have a temperature check or barometer

for the organization's appetite for acceptable risk. Ensure you have put the risks in the right context i.e. is it a risk of spending money ineffectively, risk of upsetting customers or partners, risk of being wrong about results, risk of breaking an experience or initiating downtime and disruption of business. Balance being paralyzed by the risks with getting acceptance of the potential risks ahead of time.

6. Take comfort that even in cases where you have crossed "t's" and dotted "i's" anything that could go wrong will go wrong if you are fortunate enough to work in a learning organization then you can be assured that when the inevitable goes wrong you have the mechanisms in place to learn from them quickly and can do so in a "safe" environment per point #1.

7. Finally, inherent in the commonly used phrase "ask for forgiveness vs. asking for permission" is the knowledge that there are many stories of innovation that have come out of spectacular failures or pivots and the reward in those cases far outweighs the challenges from the failure.

The business world has many stories of products that because of failures for example Bubble Wrap was supposed to be cool new textured wallpaper. It failed at that and they tried to market it as insulation and the founders Marc Chavannes and Alan Fielding failed at that. It wasn't until IBM used it to package a computer that it found its purpose and became a success.

Planning for Evaluation and Performance Reviews

Unless you are running your own business, there are very few professions where there isn't some form of performance evaluation. I am speaking directly to the business and corporate environments not unionized environments. You can expect to be evaluated typically annually at a very predictable cadence. It is this evaluation that informs whether you get a pay raise or are promoted. In some companies, there is the notion of goals you are committing to directly. These priorities or commitments are agreed to ahead of time. If you are lucky you will work in an environment where you can provide input into your commitments and there are many factors that contribute to your commitments:

1. You can set your commitments based on what you did last year and project improvement or increases based on growth trends or an estimate of the impact of improvements.

2. You can set new commitments based on a projected level of growth or penetration into a market.

3. You can set commitments based on your capacity or level of productivity.

4. You can set commitments based on the projected output of additional resources.

5. You can set commitments based on projection of gains e.g. revenue or sales from a new channel, partnership, process etc.

Regardless of the factors used to set your commitments, experience has taught me to set yourself up for success by considering the following:

1. Commit to things that are directly within your control. Where you are not in control try to ensure you are clear where you are responsible for delivering a result vs. where you are contributing or supporting driving results.

2. Commit to results that you can measure and optimize in a timely cadence.

3. Do not only articulate what you are going to deliver but understand how you are going to deliver with the dependencies you have because most times you will be working as part of a team.

4. Set delivery timelines and understand the milestones to getting your work done and build in regular check-points to ensure that you are tracking your progress.

5. Before you begin each year, document what the end of the year looks like. Detail and visualize what success looks like.

6. Build in and aim for stretch targets. Psychologically what research has shown is that if you shoot for your exact commitments you are likely to fall short vs. if you shoot for stretch goals you are likely to hit your actual goals.

7. Balance is key as you try to not to over promise but also ensure that you are not setting your goals so low that it is perceived that you are "padding" or purposely underestimating the numbers which can viewed as cheating.

Continuing Education and or Side Hustles

The last aspect of risk that I'd like to address is something that I have noticed about high performers over the years of working in corporations. High performers within a corporation usually also have something going on outside of work that can give them an edge in the workplace. Here are a few examples I have seen:

- Getting more formal education e.g. getting their MBA
- Upgrading their skills through getting certification or training in a capability
- Taking classes on Udemy.com, Lynda.com and the like
- Participation in a Professional association related to their field

- Participation in things like Startup Weekend or Hackathons
- Attending conferences and learning from peers, competitors and businesses in other industries
- Consulting in their field to small businesses
- Starting a small business or startup

The most innovative companies have recognized that encouraging moonlighting and being proactive about allowing corporate workers the flexibility to do engage in these activities can only be beneficial to the corporation. What is key for you as the employee is to use what you are learning outside of the company where it makes sense to do so in your day to day job. In my own career because I did not have any formal institutionalized training in marketing everything I have ever learned about marketing I have either learned by doing on the job or learned by doing on my own side hustles. Quite often before I bring a new capability into the company I will test it out on my own business and then I can confidently speak to whether it makes sense to pilot. Virtually every new marketing capability I have been responsible for driving in the corporations I have worked in I have tested outside of the company. I have also found conferences to be gold mines to get a sense of where technology is going and to get ahead of how it will impact my job or company. I have chosen over the years to be transparent and speak openly of things I am testing or have learned. I share with my peers and leadership and have found that people will then look to you to participate in brainstorms when the company is looking to solve big business problems or they will look to you to lead pilot programs. It also helps in ensuring you are never sucked into stagnation or a company bubble because you are always working inside but looking forward and outside. You will find that you are more apt to pay attention to what your competitors are doing or to notice young upstart companies in your field that are gaining traction. I have also found that watching other industries that may have no relation to the corporation you work for can surface new practices that may apply that give your business an edge. Though I have worked for years in the serious tech enterprise field as a marketer I have found that watching the porn, gambling and retail industries has been a solid way of anticipating changes and innovations to how technology will impact how the company will go to market.

I purposely wrote about continuing education and side hustles in the risk section because though the benefits far outweigh the risks there are some risks you may encounter depending on the type of organization you work for and their policies on moonlighting as well as how progressive your manager is. Here are some things to watch out for:

1. Make sure you understand your company's moonlighting policy and ask people about it if you have any questions or are unclear about it in any way.

2. Check your company's policies on continuing education in some cases they will reimburse you for the cost of taking the training.

3. Sometimes you might have a manager or teammates who are petty and may get jealous of your new certifications or education that makes you more qualified on paper. Use your EQ, NVC and discretion to look for negative reactions.

4. Be data driven when you suggest new practices and do not get emotionally invested in "shiny new objects" let the data do the talking.

Risks as An Entrepreneur

Remember these reasons why people tend to get promoted within a corporation?

Driving increased sales

Saving the company money

Making the company more efficient

Making more customers happy, loyal, advocates

Increasing the speed

Reducing mistakes

Improving outcome rates

Finding a new revenue channel

Finding new markets and customer bases

Enabling new tools, practices or capabilities

Making teammates better

Enabling data insights that the business can use

They also tend to be areas of focus why Entrepreneurs start their own businesses. Quite often it is finding a problem that needs solving or a unique and differentiated way of doing something that compels people to entrepreneurship. But like intrapreneurship in the corporate world, each of these endeavors involves risk and stepping out of your comfort zone. Inherent in entrepreneurship IS risk. When you look at the notion of "Doing More" as it relates to entrepreneurship again we find parallels to intrapreneurship:

1. Organizational intelligence in entrepreneurship can be translated to having domain expertise, understanding your ecosystem and the competition.

2. Clarity on your goals in entrepreneurship is represented in your pitch and business plan. Investors and stakeholders look for you to have a measurable plan to achieve your goals.

3. Knowledge and adoption of the most modern tactics that people in your profession are using in the context of

entrepreneurship is obvious as this is amongst the levers you will use to leapfrog the competition and is represented in how disruptive your idea and execution is.

4. Use of data to give you an edge in prioritizing your focus on the biggest opportunities in the context of entrepreneurship this is represented in your market research and work you do to achieve product and market fit.

5. Grit – Successful entrepreneurs tend to have resilience that drives them to push through obstacles that under normal circumstance would stop others. This is even more pronounced in the context of entrepreneurship. It goes without saying that there will be many challenges as an entrepreneur so having grit is key to managing risk as an entrepreneur.

When you look at the principles of intrapreneurship in the entrepreneurship you will find that naturally these principles are derived from the characteristics easily recognized in Entrepreneurs:

INTRAPRENEURSHIP	ENTREPRENEURSHIP
Come to work each day willing to be fired.	There is no fall back or Plan B you must go all in on committing to your business. Have skin in the game investing your time and money.
Circumvent any orders aimed at stopping your initiative.	You will hear more no's than yes. You will run into gate-keepers when you are an entrepreneur too.
Do any job needed to make your project work	As an entrepreneur you will wear many hats there is no single

regardless of your job description.	set job description when you are in startup stage.
Find people to help	Build a team.
Follow your intuition about the people you choose, and work only with the best.	You will be confronted with decisions around out-sourcing, finding founders, advisors, taking VC funding, giving equity etc. and in the decision-making, process your intuition will factor in as a guiding force.
Work underground if you can. Once the higher ups find out it triggers the "stops" from the risk averse in the corporation	Bootstrap for if you can. Build an MVP.
Never bet on a race unless you are running in it.	Build a business around a problem you are intimate with or in a domain you have expertise.
Remember, it is easier to ask for forgiveness than for permission.	Use growth hacks, be scrappy, use existing software
Be true to your goals, but be realistic about the way to achieve them.	Set and track milestones, iterate your way to the end state.
Honor your sponsors.	Honor your supporters

Ask for advice before asking for resources.	Get advisors. Gain traction before asking for funding.
Express gratitude	Thank early adopters be grateful for early supporters.
Build your team, intrapreneuring is not a solo activity	Build your team entrepreneuring is not a solo activity
Share credit widely	Share credit with your team, customers, partners, sponsors and advisors.
Keep the best interests of the company and its customers in mind, especially when you must bend the rules or circumvent the bureaucracy.	Be customer obsessed. Be transparent.
Don't ask to be fired; even as you bend the rules and act without permission, use all the political skill you and your sponsors can muster to move the project forward without making waves.	Customers can fire you. Act accordingly.

With regards to failure in entrepreneurship all the principles that were true in intrapreneurship apply and can be reiterated verbatim:

Understanding what went wrong is much more valuable and productive than figuring out who is to blame. In trouble-shooting or in doing post mortem's try to take people out of the equation and simply look at steps in the process or steps in the experience. There are some cases where much can be learned if people involved understand that there will be no negative repercussions for mistakes or unforeseen issues.

Conversely there are certain actions in specific industries where not adhering to rules and regulations does deserve severe consequences. But what is key being that the compliance checks are well socialized and widely communicated as standard practice BEFORE anyone takes risks with new initiatives and practices. For example, in certain industries putting customer data at risk is unacceptable and so that is something that should always be checked before a new initiative goes live. In certain industries taking short-cuts on quality or best practices that put human beings in danger of injury or death.

I have been fortunate to have worked at companies where the mantra of "Failing Fast" has been internalized and how that typically plays out is designing pilot programs or tests to roll out in phases minimizing a scope small enough to get statistically representative results before rolling out more broadly.

Having said that do not launch pilots in perfect conditions. Conduct pilots in the real conditions because there is no perfection in the real world. Plan for the lowest common denominator. Design your tests for the worst circumstances e.g. little to no service, old computers or people who are not tech savvy etc. Mimicking real world conditions allows you to surface real world issues.

Plan for failure ahead of time and have the potential risks documented when you are proposing an initiative or a risky project this allows you to anticipate failure, set expectations and have a temperature check or barometer for the organization's appetite for acceptable risk. Ensure you have put the risks in the right context i.e. is it a risk of spending money ineffectively, risk of upsetting customers or partners, risk of being wrong about results, risk of breaking an experience or initiating downtime and disruption of business. Balance being paralyzed by the risks with getting acceptance of the potential risks ahead of time.

Take comfort that even in cases where you have crossed "t's" and dotted "i's" anything that could go wrong will go wrong if you are fortunate enough to work in a learning organization then you can be assured that when the inevitable goes wrong you have the mechanisms in place to learn from them quickly and can do so in a "safe" environment per point #1.

Finally, inherent in the commonly used phrase "ask for forgiveness vs. asking for permission" is the knowledge that there are many stories of innovation that have come out of spectacular failures and pivots and the reward in those cases far outweighs the challenges from the failure.

Lastly in the last section we talked about side-hustles and moonlighting. When you transition to your side hustle becoming your full-time job…it's go time but before you do that you might want to use the guidelines provided in the book "Startup Opportunities: Know when to quit your day job" by Brad Feld and Sean Wise to assess whether you are ready to quit your day job. This is ultimately the 1st risky decision you will make and you can manage that risk by getting some guidance from this book and using the following checklist they give in the last chapter. (Wise, 2015)

Quit your day job readiness checklist: paraphrased

- ✓ Are you crazy obsessed with your business idea?
- ✓ Do you have the skills to bring the business idea to reality?
- ✓ Does your idea solve a need vs. a want?

- ✓ Do a lot of people have this problem?
- ✓ Is your offering better than what exists today?
- ✓ Do you accept that you will be leaving the safety net of a 9-5 paycheck?
- ✓ Do you have a plan to reach your customers?
- ✓ Do you have 6 months' worth of living expenses and capital to run the business?
- ✓ Do you have the people and roadmap to build a minimal viable product?
- ✓ Are you prepared to be both the CEO and the gofer and work hard at it?

If you don't answer yes to these questions you might not be ready to quit your day job. And answering yes to these every day when you have quit are what keeps you in the game.

CHAPTER 4

Rewards

I wanted to try to unpack the idea of rewarding work which as you can you can see from the quotes below can be defined as many ways as there are people but there are some common themes.

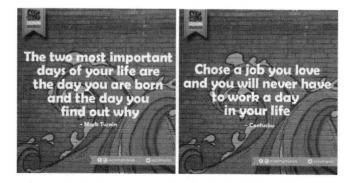

Purpose

In our world of trendy buzz words, quotes, life guru's, meme's and everyone having advice to give and sharing their opinions there are so many ways people think about what makes work rewarding. It is interesting because it can sometimes feel like only certain types of jobs deserve the "rewarding" or "purposeful" badge for example you'll hear people say things like "we're not curing cancer" or "it's not rocket science" which implies that there are certain jobs that have more value than others. I reject this and believe that everyone can either:

- Find dignity in putting in a solid day's work and being paid fairly for it
- Put their talents and abilities to a job that fits or needs those skills
- Find work that impacts people's lives or businesses positively

For example, when I think about my own profession as a Marketer in July of 2014 I published a post on Linkedin which I will reprint here as an example of how I find purpose in my profession.

> *"The Purpose Driven Marketer" "I recently had the pleasure of listening to Aaron Hurst talk about his new book "The Purpose Economy". Mr. Hurst posits that we are currently in the midst of a shift from "The Information Economy" which has been driven by advances in technology that shifted us from the previous "Industrial Economy"...and that we are now shifting to "The Purpose Economy" The signs of which are evident in the emergence of things like the sharing services, maker communities and companies taking more intrinsic approaches to social responsibility. (Hurst, 2015)*
>
> *There were so many gold nuggets in his talk but what stayed with me was the very simple notion that purpose driven people have a specific approach to work that has a direct effect on their job satisfaction and consequently probably their long-term performance.*
>
> *Quite simply people approach work one of 3 ways (1) it's a job (2) it's a career (3) it's a calling. Mr. Hurst puts forth with some compelling examples the idea that this shift to the Purpose Economy is being driven by people who approach their work as "a calling"*
>
> *This led me to think about the notion of a purpose driven marketer.... How does a marketer who approaches their work as a calling operate?*
>
> *Here are a few things you might look for when trying to spot a purpose driven marketer:*

Craftsmanship & Caring - I loved Aaron's use of the word "craftsmanship" because it implies not only knowledge and expertise but care...It also implies someone who is always learning, striving for quality and excellence and my favorite... is accountable for their work. Craftsman is such a juicy word and a marketer who is a craftsman is a student of the discipline but more important can do what they are directing others to do .... not just marketing theory and strategy but experience from executing. It sounds so simplistic but you'd be surprised at how many marketers are overseeing digital and social activities but have no digital and social footprint themselves. Or have never actually executed a self-serve campaign. On the agency side, you'd be surprised at how many creative pitches I have heard where it is clear they never actually signed up for the product or haven't really gone deep into the category to understand the nuances of the customer experience that will make the difference between a good or great Ad. This is particularly important in BtoB marketing where you are marketing products that are virtually on par with the competitor technically and it is essentially up to marketing to shift perception and drive consideration. A craftsman goes deep into their own discipline and into the ecosystem surrounding the product or service they are marketing.

A scientist rather than a CMO - Mr. Hurst notes that in the Purpose Economy the model of Learn - Earn - Return is outmoded. The notion of getting to the top when you have paid your dues and working your way up politic-ing along the way is passé in the new economy. The Purpose driven marketer will be recognizable because their career path is likely zigzagged as they have been propelled from interesting project to the next with not much regard for their title/role or the road to the C-suite. You'll find that they have likely applied their craft to many industries or audience segments validating their foundation in marketing truths along the way. I loved Seth Godin's recent post about his Thirty Years of Projects that he may have very well renamed Thirty Years of Purpose. The disregard for title-chasing allows a purpose driven marketer to not only validate foundational principles of marketing in various contexts but also discover new ways to innovate in marketing working the adaptability muscle which makes them impactful in any organization. I am fortunate to have worked directly with a few I'd put in this category for example a marketer I so admire went from marketing for eBay to Moo.com to Wool and the Gang and I have no doubt she is on the bleeding edge of what is working in marketing. From her I learned audience segmentation before they called it audience segmentation, with her we hacked re-targeting before the technology even existed. We hacked real-time creative optimization and personalization way before there were businesses who have built services around the capability all impossible without

89

data. We were doing data-driven merchandising and advertising before it was a buzzword.

Value creation - Aaron Hurst talks about people who approach work as a calling seeing their work as value creation. The purpose driven marketer doesn't just do advertising. They will be recognizable because these marketers also build products, tools, services, programs they leave the company with tangible assets. Again, I have been fortunate to work with people I would put in this category who look beyond their job description... they are always the ones who take an all up view of the business and look for gaps in the sales & marketing technology infrastructure or in the user experience and ultimately build assets that the company can leverage beyond their tenure. These are the types of marketers who can transform an organization because to add value they take the time to understand the funnel end to end and all the ways customers are touched and seek to improve upon them. A bit of this related to the characteristic of "Job crafting" that Aaron Hurst calls out in his book. People who approach their work as a calling craft their job to fit their purpose. Which is why these folks will sometimes be perceived as quirky or the rebel who is always "going rogue" or sometimes their job title doesn't quite adequately represent what they do.

Revenge of the Nerds - I'm not sure if Aaron speaks to this in his book but this is my own personal observation. Over my 20 years marketing I have been mentored by many talented marketers but some of my favorites have been the introverts disguised as extroverts... I think this is partly because so much of what we do as marketers requires selling to leadership, stakeholders or clients to get buy-in to take an approach to advertising. And most had come up in an era where the "squeaky wheel" got the attention or where salesmanship relied more on presentation performance rather than data.... Aaaah data!!! :) I personally cannot say enough about how much I adore this new era where marketers can lead with data and let it speak for itself. In a recent HBR article Why Marketing Needs More Introverts Eddie Yoon makes the bet...

"...the best marketers of tomorrow will likely be far more introverted than the average marketer is today. I would even argue that marketing needs more introverts—people who will spend more time listening than talking, reflecting deeply on meaning, and building fewer, deeper relationships." (Yoon, 2015)

He also says "...the top 10% of highly engaged consumers who can drive 50% of category profit—will continue to increase in importance and determine which brands win and which don't. Super consumers have always been important, but finding them is now easier than ever via traditional marketing, digital marketing, and geographic/local marketing. This creates more time to engage in a deeper conversation with a few key consumers, something that introverts by nature prefer. Reflecting on fewer, deeper discussions increases the likelihood of uncovering emotional and life aspirational insights—the ones that create real pricing power."

Sure, he makes a lot of general assumptions inspired by the Susan Cains book "Quiet" but I find it interesting and in a way connected to the Purpose Economy because it is in an environment where purpose is cultivated that I believe introverted leaders will shine because of the insights they will bring to the table.

You can always tell when you encounter a purpose driven marketer - together you challenge yourselves, you fearlessly experiment, you innovate, you let the data speak and you are both a student and a teacher...your purpose translates to passion and passion is the fuel for life and good work."

3 years later I find I believe what I wrote even more so than ever that you can crush corporate if you find purpose in your work. And that you can define what is rewarding for yourself.

Colleagues & Partners

Another factor for you to consider as you think about the rewards of work are the people you work with. These are the people you spend most of your life with. Apparently, the average person will spend approximately 90,000 hours at work over their lifetime. Most of us will spend more time with the people we work with than we do with our families so the impact our co-workers can have on our well-being and careers is significant. Over the years, I have recognized and accepted that you cannot expect to get along with everyone but you can strive to contribute to an environment where there is mutual respect. Looking back at 30 years of working I have found that the times when I have not been in a respectful environment with either an individual or in general with the team the core reason has been a lack of trust. Trust in my opinion is central to a healthy workplace. It doesn't matter who or how senior or junior the person is if you trust them it builds respect and loyalty and as a result you feel supported and safe to be yourself.

One of the best ways to engender trust is to be trustworthy yourself. The very simple definition of Trustworthy is "able to be relied on as honest or truthful." The synonyms are simple and clear and can provide insights into workplace examples: reliable, dependable, honest, honorable, upright, principled, true, truthful, as good as one's word, ethical, virtuous, incorruptible, unimpeachable, above suspicion; responsible, sensible, levelheaded; loyal, faithful, staunch, steadfast, trusty, safe, sound, reputable, discreet, informal, on the level, straight-up.

Here are a few things to watch for to ensure you build trust with your co-workers:

1. **Reliable| Dependable| As good as one's word**
   a. Watch out for: Your actions don't match your words. Saying things to people's face but doing something different when they are not around. Over promising and under delivering. Not delivering or communicating in a timely manner. Do what you say you are going to do.

2. **Honest| Straight-up|Upright|Truthful**
   a. Watch out for: Making up an answer or dancing around it instead of just saying "I don't know, but I will find out". Being honest if you are not able to do something. Speaking up when you don't understand something or see a problem and not waiting till it's too late to do anything about it.

3. **Incorruptible| unimpeachable**
   a. Watch out for: Cutting corners. Not following safety rules and regulations and putting others

in potential danger or impacting quality. Stealing or cheating the company on things like expenses. Being noncompliant industry standard rules or company compliance guidelines.

4. **Loyal | Faithful | Staunch**

   a. Watch out for: Backstabbing, Politicking, Protect your team. Speak up for team mates and your leaders when it appears others are targeting them. Address things with people directly first instead of having them hear you have an issue from other people. Give people a chance to address an issue before you escalate up the chain. They will do the same for you because things will always go wrong.

5. **Honorable | Principled**

   a. Watch out for: Blaming when things go wrong or as it is sometimes called "throwing people under the bus". Accept responsibility when things are your fault and look for solutions quickly. Apologize and say sorry before you are pressured to do so.

6. **Ethical**

   a. Watch out for: Discriminatory behavior, racist or sexist talk. Do not be that person who makes the workplace a hostile environment for others.

These are a few examples of things to watch out for that can affect the level of trust people put in you and diminish the likelihood of you finding rewarding professional relationships at work. There are a set of behaviors that when you read them seem obvious but when you are in the workplace you will be surprised how challenging it can be to be consistent. But not doing so are like a thousand tiny razor cuts that impact how people feel about working with you.

- **Being Late** - If you develop a pattern of walking into meetings late, joining calls late it causes unnecessary stress for your team mates especially if you are a key decision maker or person they need to consult with. They never know if you are going to show and when. It can be viewed as if you do not care or a being disrespectful even if your issue is just bad time management. Tip: Join calls or arrive to meetings 5 mins ahead of schedule. Use technology to set reminders. Tell people when you have a hard stop and need to get to the next meeting. Set the tone as a manager and start meetings on time and people will follow suit.

- **Not listening actively in meetings** - I have found that this is surprisingly hard to do consistently because we become good multi-taskers. We type as people are talking to us and we check our mail during presentations. Again, we may not have bad intentions but when you think about the time you put into presentations or when you are the person on the other end speaking and no-one is actively listening it can be demotivating.

- **Being defensive** - there will be many times you will be given feedback or something will be written in an email or something will be said on a call that you misinterpret or gets you upset. Rather than reacting you will save yourself a lot of drama by assuming the goodwill of person and getting clarification before you lash out defensively.

- **Not sharing Credit** - If other people worked on something with you share the credit. Never take credit for work you or your team didn't do. Highlight those who drove a project or really were responsible, also thank those who removed roadblocks, helped troubleshoot, accelerated timelines etc.

- **Being Negative** - there are always going to be aspects of the job that suck people don't need to be constantly reminded. It is better to be solution oriented and when things are beyond your control focus on the things that are in your control. Point out what is working even as you are looking to fix what isn't working. Particularly in high-performance, high stress environments having an authentically optimistic approach helps energize your team mates to push through. The phrase "Be the change you want to see" may be cliché but it is universally true in most situations that you can model the behavior you would like to see changed.

- **Being formal or serious 24/7** - It is ok to be ambitious, driven and on task but also recognize and allow for moments when your teammates and colleagues may need to relax and be social.

Even though we are not at work to make friends or we cannot expect to like everyone, it is at your workplace where you might find yourself a business partner or lifetime friend or even life partner and those are real rewards.

Managers and Mentors

In my experience, there are two relationships that can make or break the trajectory of your career:

Manager - this is the person you directly report to. They are the person who can give a reason to stay at the company even when the rest of the company sucks and they are also the person who can make your life a living hell even when the company is great. They are the ones who will evaluate your work and provide recommendations for promotions, bonuses and salary increases. They are the person who provides a reference should you want to leave the company. They are also the person who can put in a word should you want to move within the company and can even put your name forward for a role. They are also sometimes the person who approves attendance to conferences, taking certifications or education reimbursements. They will also be the person who must take responsibility when you do something wrong. They are also often the person who recommends who should be laid-off and who should stay.

Mentor - sometimes this can be also your manager or a former manager who you can go to for career advice or guidance. Sometimes they are someone more senior in a company who has a role that you are working towards achieving. Sometimes they are someone whose career you admire and respect and would like to emulate or learn from. Sometimes they are someone from a similar background who has reached the pinnacle in their career that you want to learn from. They can give you guidance on how to navigate the company or create a blueprint for how you can reach your goals.

Hitch your wagon to a Star

I specifically wanted to write about managers and mentors in the chapter on Rewards because when you find a good manager and or mentor it can be an extremely rewarding experience. You will know when you have found a good manager because you will want to "Hitch your wagon" to their star. I love the phrase "Hitch your wagon to a star" which when originally said meant you should always aspire to do great things. My personal interpretation is that you should always align yourself with people who aspire to do great things and are doing great things in an organization. If that happens to be your manager or mentor, then you are very lucky but if it is not then you should look for another manager or mentor. Do not waste your time on a team where the manager lacks ambition or is someone you cannot learn from.

Here are some of the signs you have a great manager:
1. They want to teach you everything they know.
2. You can openly share your ambitions and feel supported even encouraged.
3. They think you are capable of more than you think you are capable of.
4. They back you up when you have messed up and give you guidance to correct the mistake.
5. They coach you on your weaknesses.
6. They give you stretch goals but ones that are mostly aligned to your interests and strengths.
7. They remove roadblocks and fight for resources to set you up for success.
8. They acknowledge and reward your work.
9. They are willing to let you go and grow.
10. They bring you along for the ride when they go and grow.

These are the kind of managers and mentors you should hang on to for dear life. If they ask you to go with them when they get promoted do not hesitate to go. And reciprocate the rewarding relationship by being a star employee yourself.

You are your own reward but you can also be the kind of employee that your manager or mentor just loves.

Here are several ways you can be an employee your boss just loves:

1. **Not being a problem child** - On every team there will be people that the manager trusts to deliver and the people that the manager must babysit. Be the former. There will be people that others are constantly

complaining about or escalating issues. Don't be that guy or gal.

2. **Handling petty issues** - There are categories of things that the boss needs to know about and then there are things that they should never be bothered by. It is a sign of maturity for you to be able to be discerning and know what to handle on your own.

3. **Giving a heads up** - Protecting your boss and alerting them when there are issues that could impact them. Ensure your boss is never blind-sided by something you may have done or if someone is trying to undermine the team.

4. **Making them look good** - Your good work, innovative thinking and results ultimately make your manager look good. There is nothing wrong with your manager highlighting the team's work and getting accolades for work you have done when they are the kind of manager who shares credit and rewards the work.

5. **Engage and Don't leave them hanging** - Quite often your manager will look for ideas from the team. Be an asset to them by engaging and always having something to contribute.

6. **Come with solutions** - when you escalate do not just list the problems and rant at your manager but come with recommendations and solutions

7. **Don't pander be honest** - You will not always agree with your manager and may have valid reasons. Speak up and do not be afraid to point out when you are unhappy with something. No manager can read your mind and over time they will come to respect that you may be able to provide them a different POV.

8. **Realize they are just another human being** - there will be times when your manager does something disappointing. Judge them on the totality of your relationship over time not one time lapses.

9. **Present a united front** - It is a sign of maturity knowing when to back-up your manager in public and when to point out something they may have mis-stated or misrepresented or are just plain wrong about. Use your EQ to determine whether you are ride or die.

10. **Stay classy and connected** - There will be times when you must say goodbye. Your manager or mentor moves on ensure they know the impact they have had on your work life. There might be times when your manager must fire you or lay you off. Understand when there is nothing they could have done and stay classy, keep in-touch because you never know when your paths will cross again. They will always remember that you made a hard thing to do easy for them.

Stop the Soul Crushing

So, let's address the notion that working for a corporation is soul crushing work. Well I am sure it can be if you are operating like someone has a gun to your head. What this usually means is that your current job is not a good fit. For most of you there are a plethora of options and directions you can take when designing the career you would like to have. Yes! You can design not only the career you want and the lifestyle you want. The key is to recognize when you might be in a soul crushing workplace.

Typically, Soul Crushing is symptomatic of the following things:
- Where you are not using your best talent or skills
- Where you are not improving your skills
- Where you cannot see the impact of your work

- Where your work is not valued
- Where you are not set up for success

Sometimes you are going to want to look for the following key things that can be tell-tale signs:

How tech savvy is the place?

You are going to want to look for clues that the place you are working is truly operating in the age of the internet. Not all these things are red flags but a place that is still using old school technology typically hasn't automated a lot of the repetitive tasks in a job that can suck out the joy out of your work. **These are sometimes the tell-tale signs that your company is behind the times.**

Are they still using fax machines?

Do they give you a printed check instead of Direct Deposit?

Is there a thing called a punch clock in the building?

They don't have Wi-Fi

Do they firewall so you cannot surf the internets :)?

Do they make you sign up for vacation a year in advance?

Did HR hand you a binder that is their company handbook?

Did they say huh?! When you asked if they have remote workers?

Are they still using old operating systems and haven't upgraded?

Do you have to pay for your healthcare then file a reimbursement?

Do you have to bring a doctor's note to use sick days?

Telephones...just kidding...kinda

Filling out forms to get stuff done

The point is not so much about these specific things listed but it is more about how much of day is spent on crap repetitive or administrative tasks that have nothing to do with your job and could be automated or eliminated by technology. You can design your lifestyle by watching for the companies that are still stuck doing too many menial tasks that rob you of the ability to be more creative or strategic.

Does the company allow workers to work remotely? Not every company is able to do this and it doesn't always make sense for every business but it is a telltale sign of a company that has evolved beyond time constraints, geography and has a mature understanding of how professionals can deliver work even when they are working outside a cubicle.

Does the company have a dress code? Most adults can use common sense and understand when it makes sense to be formally dressed and for some businesses it makes absolute sense to be suited up. You can design your lifestyle by knowing which companies to avoid if you would rather be in your flipflops and cargo shorts. No one is forcing you to choose a path so when you do choose a path do so knowingly. And it is best to be yourself but your glossiest self when you interview with a company. I am a reasonably flamboyant person or I'd like to think I dress with some flair so when I have important meetings or interviews I will dress in a neutral classic black dress but I might have a unique necklace or style my hair in a unique way. I do this because I do not believe you should mask your personality to get a job. Remember you are interviewing the company not the other way around. You should be asking yourself four questions:

- Can I see myself dressing up every day to come to work here?
- Are they ready for me?
- Can they handle all this awesomeness {point to yourself}?
- Am I cool with who I am? It is hard to have people be cool with you if you are not cool with yourself... See the self-awareness chapter and remember the role authenticity plays in building trust.

So, don't dismiss the importance of feeling comfortable in what you are wearing as you are expected to be your most creative and innovative. So, if wearing a suit puts you in your flow then by all means wear one. If platform boots are your thing, then wear them.

I love this blog post that Mark Cuban multi-billionaire entrepreneur wrote way back in 2011 on the topic of wearing suits to work. The blog post is titled "Why I Don't Wear a Suit and Can't Figure Out Why Anyone Does!" I like this post because in it you see that he gets bolder the richer he gets. And therein lies where you need to use some common sense. Remember what I stated in the "Reality" section? If you don't work you won't eat. And if in order to eat you need to suit up then suit up. Cuban recommends a common-sense approach which I have seen a lot of my colleagues use as follows:

Cubans common sense rule:

"With our new business, I decided that I would have to wear a suit, but would modify the rule so that I would only wear a suit when someone I was selling to was wearing a suit. If they were selling to me, I didn't care if they were wearing a tux. I was going to go comfortable and not wear a suit.

Mark Cuban ends his post with some thoughts for CEO's:

"If you are a CEO, are there not better things your employees could spend money on than multiple suits, ties, dress shirts, dress shoes, dress socks, dry cleaning, and all the other associated costs? Gee, no suits would be the same as giving your employees a tax-free raise. Think that might make them happy? Or do employees consider having to spend money on suits a perk? Now I understand some people think wearing a suit provides them with a certain level of stature. It gives them confidence. It helps them feel good about themselves. Well let me be the first to tell you that if you feel like you need a suit to gain that confidence, you got problems. The minute you open your mouth, all those people who might think you have a great suit, forget about the suit and have to deal with the person wearing it." (Cuban, 2007)

You'll recognize when you read the full post that he certainly got to a place where he had the privilege to have an attitude and do something about having to wear a suit.

Another person who has gotten a lot of flak going against the so called corporate standard dress code is Mark Zuckerberg. When Facebook was going through its preparation for the IPO he caused a stir out on the roadshow by wearing his T-shirt and hoodie to chat up the financial big wigs. But in this respect, he is not alone Steve Jobs was infamous for his CEO casual style choosing to wear black turtlenecks and it has been said that he chooses to do so to let the Apple products shine in contrast to him. My opinion is that there is a time and a season for when you too can stick the middle finger up to the formal dress code. Remember the chapter where I talk about "Letting your work do the talking?" This is an example where if you have built up enough credibility to wear whatever the heck you please then you too can take back the hoodie. But if you do not have a body of work that can do the talking for you, you need to be sure that nothing you do detracts from you being able to get the opportunity to show what you can do. So be strategic when you choose to stick your middle finger up. It will forever be a balance between authenticity and not compromising who you are and doing what you need to get in the door, or get a seat at the table.

Do the employees look like they are having fun while they work? Is the energy in the office positive or negative?. Remember you have to be in this work environment for 8 hours misery loves company and enthusiasm is contagious so choose where you work wisely.

---

misery loves company and enthusiasm is contagious so choose where you work wisely.

Sometimes the soul crushing has nothing to do with the job itself but circumstances surrounding the job like a long commute. You are going to be miserable if too much of your day is filled with getting to work and back. If the distance is unavoidable, you'll want to focus on companies that have thought about the commute of their employees and have provided options like busing or paying for transit cards and train passes.

Now I could go on and list a hundred things to look out for that will make you miserable at work but what is probably more useful is to give you tips to know when you have found a good fit.

1. When It doesn't feel like work - do you find yourself just cruising along in your job. Not always a bed of roses all the time but for the most part it just comes easier to you than it may for others. You can get more done than others because you are just more proficient at it.

2. When you can be you - do you find that you can just be yourself? You don't have to pretend to be something you are not. When you can be YOU you tend to be more creative because you are not stifled and are unmasked.

3. When you would do it for free - Do you find yourself consulting on the side or giving people advice in your field? Do you find yourself volunteering in the same space? That's probably a good sign that you are where you are meant to be.

4. When you talk about your work - Do you find yourself talking to others about your work or something your company is doing? Are you proud to say you work at XYZ? Are you open about what you are specifically working on? If you can easily share what you do and proudly do so. It's probably a good sign that you are where you need to be.

5. When you don't feel like the odd one in the bunch - look around you in your workplace. Do you feel like you have found your professional tribe? I'm not talking about

having to be buddy buddy with everyone but do you feel like an equal amongst your peers and can easily converse about the task at hand and not feel like you are the only one who does or doesn't know what they're doing.

Company fit + Career fit + Caring fit = You are where you need to be.

1. **Company fit** - is this the right company for you? Are you interested in what they do?

2. **Career fit** - is this the right company to develop your career and entre/intrapreneurial ambitions with?

3. **Caring fit** - is this the right company that matches to your values and what you are about? Will you be able to look in the mirror every day before you head out to work?

Flow

In an earlier part of the book I talk about the fact that you know you have the right job when doing the work feels like it comes naturally. Sometimes that comes from having enough experience, practice and skill and other times that comes from talent. When I talk about Flow what I mean is what people have commonly defined as "The Zone"

"The Flow State" flow, also known as the zone, is the mental state of operation in which a person performing an activity is fully immersed in a feeling of energized focus, full involvement, and enjoyment in the process of the activity. In essence,

*flow is characterized by complete
absorption in what one does.*

I have experienced this in my life many times quite often when I am working on a project. The hours fly by as I'm writing or working on a presentation or as I am brainstorming, creating or designing. The thoughts seem like they are just streaming out of me and I can articulate my thoughts and translate them into driving the project forward. Sometimes I'll embark on a project and fully immerse myself in the research and what tends to happen is that you start to notice things that are related and relevant to the project all around you. As you are browsing, walking around, listening, reading you become absorbed in the initiative. When you are in your work space and hours and hours can pass by and you feel totally energized with each new idea that is coming to life. It is a truly amazing feeling and can be all encompassing but highly effectively productive time. And this is the key reason why people are interested in Flow and in understanding how to get into flow. It is important that you understand that flow is not about the chaos of multi-tasking… flow is about single-tasking and really immersing yourself in the creative task at hand. One of my favorite examples of someone in the flow is the music producer Ryan Leslie. There are many videos of him in the studio singularly focused on the creative production of his music condensed into minutes what was probably hours of work. It is thoroughly enjoyable watching him at work.

Search Youtube for "Ryan Leslie in the studio" and you will see someone who has mastered how to achieve flow state. RnB/Hip Hop Producer Ryan Leslie at work and in flow. This is one of many examples but what you notice throughout his process is he is free of distractions and totally immerses himself in the production of his work and the performance as he is creating. Here is another of my favorites. Ryan Leslie in Flow creating the song (Search <u>Promise Not to Call</u>) (Leslie, 2008) (Leslie, Promise Not to Call, 2006)

It is easy to understand the concept of flow when you watch a genius artist like Ryan Leslie. But you need to understand that The Flow State is achievable for all of us even in business or as entrepreneurs.

So why is flow important to the idea of crushing it at your corporate job? I'm a firm believer in the idea of working smarter not harder in the sense of being more efficient and productive with the time you have. In the corporate world people are notorious for looking busy and even being busy but this busyness doesn't always translate to output of any value or work that is fulfilling. I like getting into Flow state because it should start with a challenging but intellectually or creatively satisfying task and you can have fun in flow. **Here are some ways you can get into flow:**

- Choose a single task you will enjoy finishing
- Make sure it is a task you have prioritized as important
- You want the task to be challenging but achievable
- Get to work in a place you can concentrate at a time you are most energized
- Eliminate distractions ...go off the grid no email and phone
- Allot a nice long block of time
- Have fun... I quite often might read my work back to myself out loud

Keep doing this until it becomes a habit that you can tap into. What is key when it comes to flow is that it is about "being present" you are not dwelling on the past and you are not focused on planning the future you are in the now and doing work that needs to be done. The other thing about flow is that this is a multi-tasking free zone. This is going into singular focus working on only doing one thing.

Mihaly Csikzentmihalyi has an academic but interesting TED talk on flow that talks about what it feels like to be in Flow. Search "Flow, the Secret to Happiness" (Csikszentmihalyi, 2004)

Rewards in Entrepreneurship

In the previous section, we talked about rewarding work while working in a corporation. When you transition to entrepreneurship it remains key to pursue your purpose with passion. Of the 4 areas Reputation, Reality, Risks and Rewards, the rewards are probably the most obvious because in most cases the act of pursuing entrepreneurship IS the reward. People quit the corporate world to:

Pursue their passion

Fulfill their purpose

Follow the opportunity to profit

And typically, the motivation is the reward of:

Independence

Freedom

Wealth

Time

Health etc.

But how do you know when it's working well? That you are doing well? In the earlier section, we talked about Company fit+ career fit + caring fit = you are in the right place. When you transition to entrepreneurship you are looking for Product to market fit or customer validation. Do you have something that enough people are willing to pay for? And once you have determined that, can you grow and sustain the growth? You answer yes to those two questions and you will likely reap the rewards that turn your startup into a corporation. Ha! Now look at who is back at a corporation. All joking aside...remember that stat that prompted this book? I believe the reward is overcoming avoiding becoming one of the 90% that have failed. To do that you need all the cards stacked for you. I believe crushing corporate plays a role in your ability to win. Your time in the corporate world building business cases to pilot new ideas and processes and the time spent to test and learn within your corporate role will give you the skills to find product market fit for your startup. The skills you learn to measure and track the key performance indicators in the corporate world will help you to design a model that enables you to do the same as a startup.

In the previous section, we talked about managers and mentors and soul crushing companies. The tables turn when you become an entrepreneur because you are now the employer. Your time in a corporation is invaluable as you build your own corporate culture because you know what it is like to have a great manager or not. You know the soul crushing mistakes companies make and can work to ensure you don't make the same mistakes. As you become an Employer the things you looked for in a company as an employee become what you try to build as an employer. How do you build a company that doesn't crush the soul? On your way to becoming a corporation the smart startups borrow from the corporation what they know works and create new and unique ways to infuse the Founder's personal values into the company culture. The work you have done around self-awareness goes a very long way to creating not only a culture that reflects your values but a brand that is authentically you. A brand that people can connect with is one of the markers of success and when you have been in the corporate world you can be confronted with doing the work that is required to decide what you stand for. When you think about someone like Tory Burch who has built a billion-dollar company after having worked for Ralph Lauren, Vera Wang, Harper's Bazaar, Zoren. She had a very definite point of view about the notion of "accessible luxury" She had a vision and took a very experimental lab approach to her merchandise development and stores. She also has a very specific idea about the company culture that wasn't as she calls it a "Bitchy Fashion Environment" She mentions it a lot when she speaks about how she thinks of the 2000+ employee company. She is very intentional about the decisions she makes and has lessons from having worked in the corporate world. She has been on record saying she wanted to create a company she would work for. That is a key part of transitioning from crushing corporate to entrepreneurship.

High performance as an entrepreneur can be honed in the corporate world. I love the story of Sarah Blakely who was a fax machine saleswoman when she started her side hustle Spanx which is now a multi-million-dollar fashion brand. What I like about her story is the sales muscle and fearlessness that is characteristic of her journey. I have no doubts that the lessons from selling fax machines door to door for 7 years fueled her grit and resilience with which she forged her transition into entrepreneurship. On leadership she talks about building a company that is customer obsessed and differentiating her culture from the typical male dominated fashion industry by infusing love in her products. The love that comes from design that is driven by people who are also the people who "have to spend all day in the clothes". Customer obsession was key to her inventions success.

Sarah's story is super interesting because of her sales tactics that she used when she was starting up the company. She talks about spending 2 years on the road going to each store that sold her products. She would go in before the store opened and rally the sales people within the store and then she'd spend the whole day at the store talking to customers and teaching them and getting feedback on the product. She was her own sales force and she then inspired and trained the in-store staff and ultimately the customers in the store became ambassadors for Spanx.

And evident in the story of the privately-owned companies Tory Burch and Spanx is the learning from the corporate world and the reward has been sustained success with the companies 14 and 16 years old respectively.

Flow - As an entrepreneur, the need to be able to get into a flow state is even heightened by the fact that you have more to do because you are wearing more hats. Additionally, the fact that you have made the leap means there are more greater risks and responsibility therefore being able to operate with peak efficiency and focus can be invaluable when you are driving towards milestones. You also need to be able to model this skill for others on your team by fostering a culture where your team has the right tools, are working on the right things and are in an environment where they can do their best work. As an entrepreneur, you are going to rely on the ability to get into flow to propel your business step by step when you need to.

In the previous section, we talked about building trust with your colleagues. I would be remiss if I did not mention the recent startups who have really bombed in the ethics department. I am not going to name names but keep in mind that a lot of these Startups started out as darlings securing millions and millions of dollars in funding only to break the trust with their investors or customers because of unethical or tactics that walked the lined and earned the perception of being sketchy. The cautionary tale that comes with the rewards of entrepreneurship is that there is also a responsibility. While at a corporation you have some protection of having checks and balances, compliance processes that keep you in check, you no longer have that as an entrepreneur and you need to elevate your diligence in this area. Enjoy the rewards but embrace the responsibility with equal vim and vigor.

CHAPTER 5

Conclusion

So why should companies care about whether or not their employees are entrepreneurial in fact some would think that it makes more sense to stifle employees desire to become entrepreneurs because of the risk of losing good people. The best corporations do what is best for their business at the end of the day ...so the question is...

- Does it make good business sense to have employees who are entrepreneurial?
- Does it make good business sense for businesses to train their employees to be good entrepreneurs?

It is also useful to ask what the consequence of not enabling intrapreneurship is for businesses. Just ask Kodak, Blockbuster, Woolworth's, Pan Am, Borders and many more major corporations we no longer talk about.

Basically, for most companies who are not paying attention the drill goes like this.:

A. The startup grows up to become a big corporation
B. The investors and board becomes conservative taking less risks

    C.   The leadership becomes more risk averse and comfortable riding past successes

    D.   The employees become less inclined to stick their necks out with innovative ideas

    E.   Company becomes complacent and gets disrupted

There are companies particularly in the tech space who have recognized this pattern and have started to re-think how they enable intrapreneurship:

Ways Companies Can Encourage Intrapreneurship

1. Change your moonlighting policy to allow employees to have side projects and encourage hackathons.

2. Be transparent with employees about the business and the open problems that need solving. Trust them with information because it makes them feel like they have a vested interest in seeing the business succeed.

3. Have a fail fast policy that lets employees feel safe to experiment without repercussions for failure.

4. Train Managers and HR to recognize the entrepreneurial DNA.

5. Train employees to have sense of urgency and be problem solvers dealing with issues quickly.

6. Reward proactive behavior and empower managers to run their departments like a small business and think like a small business.

7. Develop a leadership culture that is focused on long-term sustained growth vs. quarterly profits.

8. Allocate investment funds for ideas that are born within the company

9. Recognize and reward good ideas

10. Provide education on growth hacking and entrepreneurial thinking.
11. Embrace friendly competition through hackathons with compelling incentives

The company DreamWorks does this well. They offer their employees classes on scriptwriting and pitching and give them an opportunity to have the ideas showcased in front of the executive leadership. The ideas that have leg's get put forward for development. Some companies allocate "dabble time" or 10-20% innovation time and some set up regular cadence of hack-a-thons to engage employees to think up fresh new products or solutions.

Here are some examples of companies who encourage entrepreneurship within the company:

Adobe

Adobe Systems is a software company based in San Jose that was founded in 1982 which makes it 34 years old. The company is focused on multimedia and creativity software tools as well as rich internet application development. The company is best known for Photoshop, Adobe Reader, the Portable Document Format (PDF) and Adobe Creative Suite. Adobe is a great example of a successful startup that became a corporation and now this 34-year-old company has to figure out how to keep their 14,000 employees engaged and innovative. And if you are an employee at Adobe you have much you can learn while you are in this former startup about building a big business. One of the very intentional ways Adobe has encouraged intrapreneurship is through the development of an innovation program called Kickbox.

Kickbox in their own words:

Kickbox was developed at Adobe by building on 30 years of experience successfully innovating. We wanted to empower individual employees to follow their instincts about emerging opportunities so we created an "innovation-in-a-box" kit. Each red box contains everything we think an enterprise innovator needs, including:

Money. Each red box contains a pre-paid credit card in the amount of US$1,000. Innovators use these funds to validate their idea.

Instructions. Kickbox includes quick reference cards outlining the six levels in the red box. Each card includes a checklist of actions innovators must complete to advance to the next level.

Other innovation tools. These include scorecards, frameworks, exercises, and other materials you'll use to develop ideas.

Caffeine and sugar. Each red box includes a Starbucks gift card and a candy bar, since we all know that two of the four major food groups of innovators are caffeine and sugar!

Review:

Kickbox was started in 2015 and 1000's of boxes has been distributed to employees around the world. Adobe is a $4 + billion-dollar company and still one of the most innovative software companies. They talk about how they have made a big transition away from thinking about innovation through boot camps and hackathons that were focused on the end result to thinking about building innovators long term. They decided to think about their employees as customers and built a product "The red box Kickbox" which they distributed the boxes to them. The projects were pre-approved, funded. They started out by surveying employees and asked them what barriers to innovation were for them. They then included in the kickbox everything that removed the barriers.

Things that make this approach awesome for the employees:

- The employee is in charge the CEO of their idea
- No management supervision needed because there is a guided process

- No expense forms to file
- They prioritize motivation as step #1 they believe you cannot pay people to innovate. They help employees find their personal passion and align that motivation with the project.

Things that make this approach awesome for Adobe:

The company went from taking 6 products and spending 1 million dollars to come up with ways to innovate going to evaluating several 100 ideas for far less money and in doing that invigorating and identifying the innovators within their company.

Results:

I suspect the impact of the program goes beyond the numbers but Adobe has indicated that they had 6% get to the last stage of the process to pitch to get their idea funded.

Source: <u>Mark Randall, How We Funded 1,000 Experiments, LSC14 time mark 19:02</u>

How Adobe Crushes:

It is no surprise then that Adobe is #9 on Glassdoor's 2017 best places to work list and their CEO Shantanu Nayaren was 2016's highest rated CEO. Of the 2000 reviews on Glassdoor 89% would recommend working at Adobe to a friend and 97% approve of the CEO.

As a wannabe entrepreneur within Adobe a program like this could be invaluable to getting a good foundation of entrepreneurial skills, mindset and reality based benchmarks and practices to be mindful of with minimal risk.

MRY

What they do: MRY is an award-winning New-York based technology and creative agency. It was founded by Matt Britton in 2002 and had the leading names such as Microsoft, Coca-Cola,

Symantec, Visa and P&G as its clients. It has 500+ employees spread across its offices in New York, San Francisco, London and Singapore. It was named as one of the top 10 most innovative advertising companies in the world by Fast Company. MRY's was acquired by LBI International in November 2011 for approximately $50 Million. In 2013 MRY parent company LBI International was acquired by Publicis Groupe.

Approach to corporate entrepreneurship: MRY supports its employees by encouraging them to develop their own apps and chase their individual dreams. CrowdTap was launched because of this side hustle by an employee while he was still working at MRY. Employees are asked to create their own honest "dream resume" – their dreams may or may not overlap with their current roles at the firm. They have a company-wide week focusing on the development of mobile technology 'Mobile Week'. In one of these weeks, a group of employees released an application to develop an app that allows staff to order coffee from the in-house barista and get notifications on their mobile devices when their beverage is ready. Their logic behind this approach is if the company doesn't help its employees pursue their goals, then the employees will also not devote themselves fully to achieve the company's goals.

"Dream resume" in their own words: We ask our employees to create their "dream resume" and being completely honest in doing so. We then provide opportunities for them to develop the skill sets that bring them closer to their dream careers. For example, if an employee's dream is to become a sports broadcaster, then we offer appropriate opportunities to present in front of larger audience. Or, if someone shows inclination to be an artist, they are presented with opportunities that require working with design. Our leader's practices what they preach. When an employee wants to experiment, we don't stop but push them to go ahead and pursue their dreams. We value our young millennial generation by continually thinking about and listening to them.

Things that make this approach awesome for the employees: Employees who go beyond their normal workload to put their time and efforts into creating a new product enjoy the pride that comes with adding the accomplishment to their resume. Employees pursue their dreams, enhance their talent and build stronger resumes along the way.

Things that make this approach awesome for MRY: "Promoting intrapreneurship or entrepreneurship within a company helps MRY to keep their ambitious employees happy. This adds value to the company's employer brand and giving them a competitive advantage.

Results: CrowdTap scored more than $10 million in funding, and eventually spun off into its own company, which now has 50+ employees and $8 million in annual revenues. Over the last five years, MRY has had a 75 per cent retention rate.

Glassdoor Reviews of the company: MRY is rated as 3.3/5 on Glassdoor. Of the 91 reviews on Glassdoor, 51% would recommend it to a friend and 72% approve of the CEO, Matt Britton.

(Clifford, 2013) (Loper, 2015) (Leow, 2016)

Intuit

What they do: Founded in 1983, Intuit offers business and financial management solutions for small and medium businesses, financial institutions, consumers and accounting professionals. The company's product portfolio includes TurboTax, Quicken; QuickBooks; Mint.com, and more. The company also offers end-to-end solutions for online tax preparation, download products, mobile tax prep, mortgage interest and property tax, corporation tax, military tax etc. It is based in Mountain View, California and serves customers in North America, Asia, Europe, and Australia with offices in the United States, Canada, India, U. K., and Singapore.

Their approach to corporate entrepreneurship: Intuit follows an instructive approach for intrapreneurship. It puts employees and their passions at the core. It has built-in a supportive ecosystem to encourage their employee to innovate. Employees are given all the tools and resources to be successful in their intrapreneurial projects. There are several mechanisms in place such as Unstructured Time, Innovation Jams, Training, Lean Start-ups, Innovation Awards and Innovation Tools. Intuit uses time as a reward because it believes time is the biggest motivator for corporate intrapreneurs. Intuit gives its best business innovators three months of "unstructured" time that can be used in one big chunk or spread out over six months for part-time exploration of new opportunities. To coax people away from their everyday work, the company puts some structure in that unstructured time. Periodic multi-day hackathons are run where teams of developers present pet projects and compete to tackle specific challenges aligned with the company's broader strategy (e.g., easy, fast tax return completion) in exchange for prizes and recognition. This helps to bring intrapreneurs together in one place, allowing for cross-functional interaction, as well as allows the organization to keep innovation aimed at themes. Intuit also has a group of employees known as Innovation Catalysts Mentors – these are experts in Design for Delight. Intuit has created a flexible organizational design that enables creativity and allows swift decision making to keep the intrapreneurs progressing towards their goals.

Unstructured time in their own words: Our mission is to give great people with great ideas the time and freedom to pursue them. Employees can spend up to 10% of their time on Unstructured Time projects they're passionate about. If employees prefer, they can aggregate their Unstructured Time into contiguous blocks. Regular project planning will assume the 10% use of Unstructured Time across all employees. Our employees love Unstructured Time because it incorporates Dan Pink's 3 Elements of True Motivation - Autonomy (the desire to direct our own lives); Mastery (the urge to get better and better at something that matters); and Purpose (the yearning to do what we do in the service of something larger than ourselves). Unstructured Time can be used for three things – solving important customer problems, making our work/code environment better, and professional development.

Things that make this approach awesome for the employees:

Instead of taking short periods of time frequently, employees are encouraged to take a larger block of time, e.g. 40 hours after every 10 weeks, to focus on their unstructured time ideas.

Put together a small team of intrapreneurs who share the same traits of passion, energy and persistence, preferably with complementary skills to transform the vision into reality.

Host innovation events e.g. idea jams to add some structure to the whole thing.

Empower intrapreneurs to make some of the big decisions on their own such as whether to cut or continue their project. This sense of autonomy increases engagement.

Failure is not looked down upon. Learning from each idea is shared across the organization so that others can benefit from this and take smart risks.

Innovation catalysts are the trained volunteers who are willing to spend 10% of their time mentoring the intrapreneurs. Managers are also incentivized to recognize and support entrepreneurial behavior and experimentation.

Things that make this approach awesome for Intuit: Intuit employees now focus more on not just satisfying but delighting the customers.

Results: Since Unstructured Time was launched company-wide at Intuit in 2008, it has generated hundreds of big and small success stories including most of the company's innovative products such as SnapTax, GoPayment and ViewMyPaycheck. Within three years of the launch of unstructured time, Intuit counted $100million in new revenue from product offerings because of this program.

Glassdoor Reviews of the company: Intuit is rated as 4.3/5 on Glassdoor. Of the 2900 reviews on Glassdoor, 87% would recommend it to a friend and 97% approve of the CEO, Brad Smith.

(Upbin, 2012) (McNealy, 2011) (HBR, 2016) (Ferrier, 2014) (Intuit, 2009) (Tobias, 2016) (Kali Fry, 2015) (Glassdoor, 2017)

General Motors

What they do: General Motors was founded in 1908 by William C. Durant, Charles Mott and Frederic L. Smith and the new GM incorporated on August 11, 2009. The company designs, builds and sells cars, trucks, crossovers and automobile parts. Some of its major brands are Buick, Cadillac and Chevrolet in North America, and GMC, Holden, Opel and Vauxhall outside North America. The company is headquartered in Detroit, Michigan.

Their approach to corporate entrepreneurship: Saturn was the result of an experimental project started by General Motors in 1982. General Motors was facing tough competition from the imported cars and they realized that their old ways of working were not responding to the new challenges. It wanted to explore the idea of building a small car of superior quality and value as efficiently as possible, combining the most advanced technology with the newest approaches to management. Therefore, it launched Saturn Corporation as its entrepreneurial subsidiary. GM adopted a "clean sheet" approach pledging that they would apply free flowing mind to find new approaches and solutions to their problems and would not hinder creativity by traditional thinking and age-old practices. Saturn was organized as a collection of small, self-organizing business units. Each team managed its own budget, stock, staffing and other operational matters without intervention from senior management. The conventional hierarchical organization structure was replaced with the 'circles' to encourage interactions among cross-functional work units and build a participatory dialogue in the business. Individual rewards were tied to the overall company's performance. 20 per cent of workers' wages were to go back to GM if certain pre-determined performance goals were not met. If the goals were exceeded workers gained above the 100 per cent base salary.

In their own words: The importance of the project is evident in the wording of its announcement. Chairman Roger Smith announced Saturn as "the key to GM's long-term competitiveness, survival, and success as a domestic producer.... We expect it to be a learning laboratory," he said. "We also expect that what we learn with Saturn will spread throughout GM." He described Saturn as the key to improving every GM plant and product. From community and employee involvement in decision making, to environmentally responsible plant design, to dealers trained to avoid the high-pressure sales techniques typical of traditional car salesmen, Saturn has sought to embody a 1990s model of corporate enlightenment.

Things that made this approach awesome for the employees:
Involvement was the central philosophy of Saturn's leadership. People were involved in the decisions affecting them including product quality, work life balance and business strategy.

People feel a sense of ownership and a personal sense of duty and responsibility to make their decisions work.

Things that made this approach awesome for Saturn: As a result of the approach, absenteeism fell significantly and workers' commitment increased. Workers were acclimated to Saturn's philosophy through core courses on conflict management, consensus decision making, and team dynamics. The training program sought to promote teamwork, self-direction, initiative, and responsibility. In 1992, Saturn's success in managing human resources could be measured by the lowest absentee rate in the industry: absenteeism at Saturn was 2.5 percent, a far cry from the 14 percent at other GM plants.

Results: In 1992, Saturn produced a car ranked just behind the imported luxury cars produced by Toyota and Nissan. Saturn was successful as a "different small car" and was seen as the embodiment of General Motor's vision of modern corporate ideals. Note: The Saturn Company was one of the brands impacted by the financial crisis in 2008 and as part of GM's restructuring was closed in 2009.

Glassdoor Reviews of the company: General Motors is rated as 3.7/5 on Glassdoor. Of the 2029 reviews on Glassdoor, 73% would recommend it to a friend and 92% approve of the CEO, Mary Barra.

(Deeb, 2015) (George, 2016) (Emmanuel, 2010) (Digman, 1997) (Glassdoor, 2017)

Basecamp

What they do: 37 Signals was founded in 1999 as a technology and design company that primarily makes Web-based software. While based in Chicago, it has a remotely distributed workforce of approximately 40 people. In 2004, it developed a web-based project management tool, Basecamp. Considering the growth potential of Basecamp, 37Signals changed its name to Basecamp. Although small, Basecamp has over 7 million users, and 60 percent of the Fortune 500 companies use its products.

Their approach to corporate entrepreneurship: Basecamp allows its employees to pursue their interests outside work. The company goes to the extent of helping them pay for it by giving company's credit cards. Employees must come back and share what they've learnt with everyone else. This encourages a sense of responsibility as well as pursuit of interesting skills. Basecamp provides employees with discretionary time to pursue work-related projects. They have a standard four-day work week to help employees pursue outside interests and side hustles. Employees who have been at the company for at least a year get the option to work a four-day workweek from May to October. They feel that when people have less time, they tend to compress the work and leave out unnecessary stuff. They don't shut down the same day each week. This is achieved by managing a staggered schedule for their staff and looking at the bigger picture. There are always people available who are working while others take days off as a team. They believe that workaholics never win. Their philosophy is not to work harder but to use creativity to solve problems in easier ways. Their bestselling project management product "Basecamp" was developed when the employee was on only 10 hours a workweek. By embracing constraints, you can do great work. Don't let one part of your life consume all your time; box it up and start looking for unobvious ways to do more in less time. Basecamp wants to have interesting people at work who think creatively and pursue their passions.

In their own words: We have decided that we would help people pay for their passions, interests, or other curiosities. We want our people to experience new things, discover new hobbies, and generally be interesting people. For example, one of our employees has recently taken up flight lessons. Basecamp is helping him pay for those. If someone wants to take cooking lessons, we'll help pay for those. If someone wants to take a woodworking class, we'll help pay for that. Part of the deal is that if Basecamp helps you pay, you must share what you've learned with everyone. Not just everyone at Basecamp, but everyone who reads our blog. We expect to see some blog posts about these experiences. We give everyone at Basecamp a credit card. If an employee wants to a book or some software or you want to go to a conference, it's on us. We just ask people to be reasonable with their spending. If there's a problem, we'll let the person know. We'd rather trust people to make reasonable spending decisions than assume people will abuse the privilege by default. We also established 4-day work weeks as a standard. The key to making it work is to look at the big picture and stagger schedules.

Things that make this approach awesome for the employees: People can take Fridays and Mondays off. This gives them a three-day weekend to pursue their passions – that too on company's credit cards. When employees get to pursue their outside interests, they feel refreshed and happier.

Things that make this approach awesome for Basecamp: It allows them to attract the best talent and keep them for much longer than most tech companies can say is the average. Also, happier people are more productive, efficient and creative at work. Intrapreneurial workplace culture fosters a sense of trust between the company and employees, as well as a sense of ownership on employees' part. The sense of autonomy drives company's performance.

Results: This approach helped Basecamp to launch new projects and improvements more quickly. Forging stronger relationships with customers and incorporating customers' feedback into product improvements. For example, Noah Lorang, an employee at the company, decided to build an internal analytics dashboard to enhance company performance. He completed the project without needing to secure approval from a more senior colleague. This dashboard, which displays operations and support data, is now a tool that more than half of the company uses every day. Because of the dashboard, the customer support team was better able to manage work and email, decreasing turnaround time for support requests from several hours to several minutes in approximately one year. In January 2013, the average wait time for customer support was only 13 minutes.

Glassdoor Reviews of the company: Basecamp is rated as 3.5/5 on Glassdoor.

(basecamp.com, 1999) (Loper, 2015) (Caligiuri, 2015) (Vozza, 2015) (Sahadi, 2015) (Bihr, 2008) (Fried, 2008) (Glassdoor, 2017)

Facebook

What they do: Facebook is a social networking platform and mobile application that enables people to connect, share, discover and communicate with each other through mobile devices and personal computers. It enables people to share their photos, videos, thoughts, activities and opinions. Facebooks' major product offerings include, Instagram, Messenger, WhatsApp and others. Facebook has approximately 930 million daily active users (DAUs) who access the application.

Their approach to corporate entrepreneurship: Facebook drives intrapreneurship through "Hackathons" which promote product innovation through their engineering teams. Facebook's legendary "Like" button was conceived during one of these hackathons. Hackathons are events which bring together the engineers to collaborate in an all-night brainstorming and coding sessions on a software related project. There's just one rule for a Facebook hackathon: You can't work on the same thing that you work on during the day. Whenever any employee comes across with an open-ended, challenging and aspirational question without obvious solutions, hackathons can be organized. Either the employee himself or through an assigned team sends an invite for the hackathon to the colleagues from different teams. This is an ideal way to get their ideas rolling fast. It is open to all employees who wish to participate and even people from cross-functional team such as HR, Legal, Finance etc. also jump in. There is no limit to the number of ideas that can be put forward. Before every hackathon, an internal wiki is created where people can start brainstorming, plug their hackathon ideas and find teams to help them execute. After each hackathon, a prototype forum is held where everyone who built a project can present it to the company. Prototype forum is held a week after the hackathon. This gives sufficient time for people to refine their projects and prepare them for live demos. Each participant gets two minutes of time at the forum to present their idea and convince their colleagues why their ideas should be shipped.

Hackathons in their own words: Every couple of months, a few hundred of our engineers unleash their talents in epic, all-night coding sessions, and often end up with products that hit the internal and external versions of the site within weeks. These are Facebook hackathons, and since the first "official" hackathon in 2007, they've remained one of the most exciting opportunities people here must make a major impact in short period of time. Hackathons are a chance for engineers, and anyone else in the company, to transform the spark of an idea into a working prototype and get other people excited about its potential. We're a culture of builders, and hackathons are our time to take any idea—big or small, sane or crazy—and build it into something real for people to react to. Instead of worrying if their idea will scale for more than 900 million people, people can focus on getting their basic project up and running so the broader team can quickly iterate to make it better.

Things that make this approach awesome for the employees: Employees can use hackathons as a time to hone a new skill or work on projects where they can be exposed to unfamiliar technologies. This gives them a chance to develop and enhance their careers. It is like an informal get-together to ignite a sense of opportunity and creativity, build relationships and achieve specific outcome.

Things that make this approach awesome for Facebook: Great ideas and products come from letting employees think, experiment, and play. Hackathons can be used not just to develop new products ideas for the customers but also to tackle wider problems such as figuring out new ways of working. Hackathons serves as a focused and energizing platform for developing real solutions to real organization problems. It also creates an on-going capability to continuously improve how the organization works.

Results: Though there are no formal statistics on the "like" rate but we all are aware of how the Facebook's "Like" button affects us on a daily basis. 60% of the projects from the hacks held between December 2011 and March 2012 were shipped either internally or to people using Facebook. Good ideas get implemented quickly and influence the way forward. Some of the most-loved products and features of Facebook were started at hackathons, including Video, the Like button, Chat, Hip Hop Full-screen photos, and even Timeline. Several years ago, an intern built the "tagging in comments" functionality at a hackathon. When he presented it at the forum, everyone's reaction was the same—we couldn't believe that someone hadn't built this yet. It was shipped to 100% of users within two weeks.

Glassdoor Reviews of the company: Facebook is rated as 4.5/5 on Glassdoor. Of the 1465 reviews on Glassdoor, 92% would recommend it to a friend and 98% approve of the CEO, Mark Zuckerberg.

(Vocoli, 2014) (Pedram Keyani, 2012) (Schawbel, 2012) (Schawbel, 2013) (Ian Marcouse, 2015) (Glassdoor, 2017)

Sony

What they do: Sony Corp is a consumer electronics company with a wide set of product segments including Mobile Communications (MC), Game & Network Services (G&NS),

Imaging Products & Solutions (IP&S), Home Entertainment & Sound (HE&S), Devices, Pictures, Music, Financial Services and All Others. It is engaged in the development, design, manufacture and sale of various kinds of electronic equipment, instruments and devices for consumer, professional and industrial markets, as well as game consoles and software. It was founded in 1946 and is headquartered in Japan. For the fiscal year ending 31 March 2016, it had consolidated sales and operating revenue 8,105,712 million yen.

Their approach to corporate entrepreneurship: Earlier, Sony's corporate culture favored top-down ideas delivered from executives to engineers and designers. Due to this strategy, the company was not coming up with the new products. Therefore, it decided to reverse the direction and promote ideas bottoms up, funding them outside normal channels. PlayStation was the result of an unflinching support extended by the then CEO of the company to a junior staff member's idea of delivering a better and more powerful gaming experience than Nintendo. When senior leaders of the company show that they are open to new ideas even when they are just concepts at the beginning and put their trust in the company's employees, it results in disruptive innovations. The idea of PlayStation saw the light of the day owing to the persistence of the intrapreneur, Ken Kurtagi who fought against the corporate 'nay sayers' as well as strong backing by the Chairman Ohga who supported the entrepreneurial spirit and creativity of his employee.

In their own words: We are trying to foster a culture of 'disobedient participation' to nurture corporate entrepreneurship spirit among our employees. The top leaders meet personally with young developers to probe their ideas, test prototypes and give feedback. We have embraced crowd-funding to support the upcoming ideas. Two things are important for fostering intrapreneurial environment in the workplace – one, encouragement and support from senior management, and two, reassurance that even if the ideas fail the intrapreneurs will not lose her or his job or be "punished" in other ways.

Things that make this approach awesome for the employees: The creator benefits from a corporate setting that fosters creativity by allowing them to pursue their own projects. Employees get a chance to showcase their creative ideas and are given bigger responsibility in the company. Ken Kutaragi, earlier a sound engineer was soon rewarded for his significant good results as an intrapreneur for developing PlayStation. He was promoted to be the Chairman of Sony Computer system Entertainment (SCEI), the movie video game division of Sony Company. As Chairman and CEO, Kutaragi developed the Sony Computer System Entertainment team into a strong revenue channel for the company. In late 1996, Ken was replaced as President of Sony Computer System Entertainment and was promoted to Chairman of Sony Computer System Entertainment.

Things that make this approach awesome for Sony: The top leadership support of intrapreneurship and innovation is particularly significant in the current times when companies are grappling with a post-recessionary economy marked with slow growth as well as facing fierce global competition.

Results: PlayStation has been considered amongst the greatest new business developments and launches in business history. The financial success of the Sony PlayStation was so impressive that by 1998, the PlayStation was providing a significant percentage of Sony's operating profits. Sony's PlayStation product line has grown to be a leading movie-video game platform.

Glassdoor Reviews of the company: Sony is rated as 3.5/5 on Glassdoor. Of the 717 reviews on Glassdoor, 67% would recommend it to a friend and 90% approve of the CEO, Kazuo Hirai.

(Beda, 2011) (Swearingen, 2008) (Magida, 2012) (Kneece, 2014) (Glassdoor, 2017) (White, 2004) (Loudon, 2001)

Hubspot

What they do: HubSpot is a Boston-based marketing and analytics software company that provides a cloud-based marketing and sales software platform for businesses in the Americas, Europe, and the Asia Pacific. Its software platform includes integrated applications, such as social media, search engine optimization, blogging, Website content management, marketing automation, email, CRM, analytics, and reporting that enables businesses to attract visitors to their Websites, convert visitors into leads, and close leads into customers and delight customers. The company also offers professional, and phone and email-based support services. HubSpot, Inc. was founded in 2005 and is headquartered in Cambridge, Massachusetts.

Their approach to corporate entrepreneurship: HubSpot promotes and funds unconventional projects. This helps them to create an innovation pipeline that offsets a traditional disciplined focus on the core business. Their framework for corporate entrepreneurship challenges the basic question -- "Why do well managed successful companies repeatedly fail to create new disruptive innovations?" HubSpot has created a strong culture of entrepreneurial exploration. It follows a three-tiered approach called HubSpot's Experimentation Framework. There are three stages each with a distinct goal and approach.

Alpha – Lowering barriers to experimentation No bureaucracy, no red tape, full access to information. This stage is simply focused on enabling anyone with energy and an idea to try a new solution. Tests are run by everyone and anyone – but are generally done in spare time (nights and weekends) and with few resources. You don't need to ask permission to run these tests – and by design no one ever knows all the alpha stage experiments actively being pursued. It's open and distributed.

Beta – Determining proper funding When an experiment reaches Beta stage the 'founders' are fired from their day job and work on the experiment full time. While founders determine their own goals and metrics – these leaders are encouraged to be patient for growth but impatient for profitable economics. Like many founders these people also report to a 'board' regularly and are subject to evaluation on future funding. At its core this stage is about providing access to funding for entrepreneurial folks with new ideas and transparency/accountability into the success of those early tests.

v1 – Scaling successful experiments v1 projects have proven economics and now are looking to scale the success. Often this requires growing the team beyond the founders, building dedicated systems and developing regular tracking of core metrics. Founders with experiments graduated to v1 are now considered 'mini-CEO's' and are tasked with running their project as a start-up within HubSpot.

In their own words: Our priority is to create the kind of company that people would love to work for – one that promotes an authentic culture of happiness by empowering its employees to work towards collaborative success. We established this framework in the hope of driving innovation and empowering the entrepreneurial edges of our organization to create change. We don't wait for customers to tell us what to build. As the innovator, we must create something great that goes beyond what the customer expects from their experience with the current product. We have created teams that ran like in-house startups whether it involved putting in time outside the 9-5 to work on their side-hustle projects. As an innovator, we allow our employees to take risks and go beyond the obvious.

Things that make this approach awesome for the employees: This approach gives employees autonomy to reach their full potential by facilitating a sense of ownership. It allows the employees to take a project, run with it and own it.

Things that make this approach awesome for HubSpot: Given the space to innovate, company can stay flexible, agile and move quickly without running decisions by committee. This helps to create a culture to be proud of. It enables the company to focus on the core business without foregoing the entrepreneurial energy and creativity of the employees.

Results: This approach seems to be working. There are several successful founders who have graduated who from the program e.g. Pete Caputa with VAR program, Jordyne Wu with the Services Marketplace. HubSpot came up with two of the newest and most anticipated offerings in 2014 – Sidekick and the HubSpot CRM.

Glassdoor Reviews of the company: HubSpot was ranked in the top five in Glassdoor's 2016 Best Places to Work. HubSpot is rated as 4.6/5 on Glassdoor. Of the 389 reviews on Glassdoor, 93% would recommend it to a friend and 97% approve of the CEO, Brian Halligan.

(Edwards, 2015) (Oetting, 2015) (Coffey, 2011) (Glassdoor, 2017)

Infusionsoft

What they do: Infusionsoft provides web-based sales and marketing software to help small businesses automatically market to get more customers, grow sales and save time. Its software combines contact management, customer resource management (CRM), marketing automation, and e-commerce in a single online system; and enables users to keep track of contacts, appointments, tasks, and other things about their business in a single place. The company also provides training and support services. Infusionsoft, Inc. was formerly known as Infusion Software, Inc. and changed its name to Infusionsoft, Inc. in April 2008. The company was founded in 2001 and is based in Chandler, Arizona. It ranked #1835 on 2014 INC. 5000.

Their approach to corporate entrepreneurship: Infusionsoft encourages its employees to start a business on the side. Since their software is dedicated to serve small businesses, they give every one of their workers a license for free and invite them to use it however they like. The theory is they'll be more in tune with what customers want and need if they are users of the software themselves. In 2012, it started the concept of Dream Manager Program where they hired a Dream manager who was a full-time employee at Infusionsoft. The Dream Manager acts as a personal coach to each employee to help them envision their dreams, plan for their dreams, and hold them accountable so they effectively progress toward realizing their dreams. The Dream Manager asks them to write down one hundred dreams and eventually they pick one dream together and start to develop a plan on how to accomplish it. From there they have follow up meetings and track the progress of where everyone is at in relation to achieving their dream for the year. This was inspired from the book Dream Manager, by Mathew Kelly.

In their own words: Instead of being worried about employee turnover or even lack of dedication if everyone had their own side hustle going on, we worry about what happens if we don't train our team and they continue to stay with us. One of our core values is 'We believe in People and their dreams". These additional projects allow people to follow their passions, develop their interests and increase skills. But to make it all work, these projects should be optional. You don't want to force people to work on something they don't want to, and, conversely, you want them to take their time on the work that is most meaningful.

Things that make this approach awesome for the employees: This helps employees find fulfillment in all aspects of their life. It encourages people to break away from old ways of thinking or doing things just because they are familiar and safe. Several employees have accomplished their passions including running a marathon, developing a new app, publishing a book, getting a promotion, traveling the world and getting out of debt.

Things that make this approach awesome for Infusionsoft: They have employees who are extremely passionate about the company that they work for and are actively engaged in the workplace. This helps to keep the employees motivated and excited about their job. People tend to be more engaged when they do something they love in their workplace. As team members, share simple but significant dreams with each other. Team unity is built and a culture of dreaming is born.

Results: Infusionsoft has won many awards being a "Best Place to Work by various publications and websites.

Glassdoor Review of the company: Infusionsoft is rated as 3.4/5 on Glassdoor. Of the 137 reviews on Glassdoor, 60% would recommend it to a friend and 70% approve of the CEO.

(Jonas, 2016) (Loper, 2015) (Mayberry, 2015) (Halladay, 2011) (Morgan, 2015) (Wagner, 2016) (Infusionsoft, 2017) (Glassdoor, 2017)

Sun Microsystems

What they do: Sun Microsystems is now a wholly owned subsidiary of Oracle Corporation which is an enterprise software company that specializes in virtualization, cloud computing and end user computing. It is involved in the development, manufacturing, distribution, servicing and marketing of database, middleware, and application software worldwide. Sun Microsystems key products are Solaris, Java, MySQL and the Network File System (NFS). IT was founded in 1982 and was headquartered in Santa Clara, California (USA).

Their approach to corporate entrepreneurship: Sun Microsystems actively encourages intrapreneurship through its Advanced Development software division. When a project or a promising idea is proposed, a senior manager is specifically tasked with putting together an intrapreneurial team specifically with the task of brainstorming ideas and identifying issues. Visionaries at Sun are encouraged to come forward and share ideas, create mindshare among coworkers, and get support from management. It is often the case that intrapreneurs who have had success and a proven track record within Sun can get their projects funded quickly. Ideas often lead to significant funding and the formation of a company in startup mode for bringing the ideas to market. Sun also allows fledgling projects to operate outside established product development rules, which might otherwise handicap a startup effort. Sun's most famous project was the development of the Java programming platform led by James Gosling and Patrick Naughton. Their original task was to figure-out what would be the next big change in computer programming languages. The project, code-named Oak, started small with limited resources, but quickly grew to 15 people. In just over a year, the group had completed and delivered a prototype and a project plan. Sun trains intrapreneurial qualities among its employees by posting articles on its internal website about how to be successful and develop intrapreneurial qualities, such as: how to explain the technology to the non-technical, how to submit papers and present ideas and gaining visibility, how to get others involved, and, interestingly, how to reigning-in one's passion etc.

In their own words: We encourage our employees to be creative. Scott McNealy, founder of Sun Microsystems, exemplified this by saying "To ask permission is to seek denial."

Things that make this approach awesome for the employees: Employees find the leaders are accessible and approachable. Senior leaders are ready to back up and sponsor innovative ideas coming from employees.

Things that make this approach awesome for Sun: By seeing an opportunity and taking a quick action the company can increase its profits and market share. Sun had been able to retain employees who have proven to be extremely valuable to the company due to intrapreneurship initiatives.

Results: Within few years, Java had become one of Sun's key products. By the end of 1996, Java had nearly 100 licensees and had attracted 6,000 developers.

Glassdoor Reviews of the company: Sun Microsystems is rated as 3.7/5 on Glassdoor. Of the 1099 reviews on Glassdoor, 53% would recommend it to a friend and 64% approve of the CEO, Mark Hurd and Safra Catz.

(Kneece, 2014) (Deeb, 2015) (Swearingen, 2008) (Gall, 2006) (Phillips, 2007) (Glassdoor, 2017)

3M

What they do: 3M Company, popularly known as 3M, is a technology company headquartered in Maplewood, Minnesota, U.S. It operates in five segments – industrial, safety and graphics, electronics and energy, healthcare and consumer. With annual revenue of over $30billion, 3M employs 88,000 employees and produces more than 55,000 products worldwide. It has operations in more than 65 countries. 3M ranked #93 in the Forbes 500 List in 2016. 3M has been named one of the top ten most innovative companies in the world (3rd position) by Strategy and Price Waterhouse Coopers in its 2016 survey.

Their approach to corporate entrepreneurship: 3M has a successful intrapreneurship program known as the "Bootlegging Policy" which allows employees to spend 15% of their time working on their own ideas. 3M has also introduced another program 'Genesis Grant' which offer grants of up to $85, 000 to selected innovators to move their projects past the idea stage. Bootlegging has led to some of 3M's most successful products such as Scotch Tape and Post-it Notes. 3M supports in intrapreneurial activity in more than one ways. In addition to allowing bootlegging time for traditional product development, 3M implements two intrapreneurial approaches – Skunkworks and Pacing Programs. A skunkworks project is initiated by an employee who conceives an idea and then recruits resources from within 3M to turn it into a commercial product. Pacing Programs are company-initiated projects that focus on a few products for rapid marketplace winners. The Company provides financing, equipment and people to support such pacing programs. 3M takes a long-term approach to the new product development process by creating a culture of innovation that encourages risk-taking, tolerates mistakes and rewards achievement. Senior leaders nurture an environment of trust and openness where employees break out of their comfort zones to create truly disruptive technology.

In their own words: We provide centers and forums to our employees to pursue opportunities outside their job roles. For example, the Technical Forum, an internal society where our scientists present papers, the Technical Council for scientists to meet periodically to share knowledge and build relationships; Innovation Centers set up specifically for the purpose of exploring possibilities, solving problems and generating product ideas. We create the right environment that fosters innovative thinking. At 3M, the freedom to pursue innovative ideas is guaranteed and encouraged by the upper management. They realize that not every new program will succeed. There will be failures and acceptance of failure encourages risk taking. The simple statement of William L. Mcknight, former 3M President and CEO serves as the cornerstone for the development and enhancement of an innovative culture that has survived for more than 100 years: "The first principle is the promotion of entrepreneurship and insistence upon freedom in the workplace to pursue innovative ideas." We focus most our awards and recognition programs on new products and innovation because this reinforces our vision. We have several corporate recognition programs in place: 'Golden Step Award' – recognizes cross-functional teams that bring high quality new products to the marketplace; 'Carlton Society'-an honorary organization of individuals who have made important contributions to the progress of 3M's science and technology; 'Technical Circle of Excellence'- recognizes excellence in the laboratory during a one-year time frame; and many more.

Things that make this approach awesome for the employees: It enables employees to inculcate open-minded and visionary thinking that helps to execute projects in a deliberate and precise manner.

Things that make this approach awesome for the employer: This has helped 3M to create a creative and passionate workforce that holds the key to company's competitive advantage. It has also helped to retain employees who would otherwise leave for another company or to start their own business.

Results: Through its intrapreneurial attitude, 3M benefitted from the creative ideas that came from its employees. Scotch Tape and Post-it notes are amongst such innovative products that emerged because of its Bootlegging Policy. Today the 3M Post-it Notes sell over $100 million a year units a year and can be found in nearly every workplace and home.

Glassdoor Reviews of the company: 3M is rated as 3.7/5 on Glassdoor. Of the 1269, reviews on Glassdoor, 75% would recommend it to a friend and 85% approve of the CEO, Inge G. Thulin.

(Beda A. , 2011) (3M, 2002) (Kurtz., 2011) (CCSBE, 1996) (Lussier, 2014) (Esteban R. Brenes, 2012) (Glassdoor, 2017)

Shopify

What they do: Shopify is a provider of a cloud-based, multi-channel commerce platform catering to small and medium-sized businesses. Merchants use the software to run their business across different sales channels such as web and mobile, social media such as Facebook, Twitter and Pinterest and physical retail locations. The Company's platform provides merchants with a single view of their business and customers across all their sales channels and enables them to manage the back-end processes as an integrated back office. In 2012 it was named as one of Canada's Smartest Companies by Profit Magazine. Among the country's most innovative companies,

Shopify was crowned as Employer of the Year in 2014 by Canadian Startup Awards. In 2015, Shopify had 140,000 stores with $3.7 billion in sales.

Their approach to corporate entrepreneurship: Shopify gives freedom to its employee to pursue their side-hustles. Most people working at Shopify were entrepreneurs when they got hired and now have their own online stores. Shopify hires entrepreneurs and then encourages and supports them to pursue their own things. The company offers a standing offer of $250 to any employee interested in starting a business using the platform. There are several employees who leveraged this internal program to seek personal goals. For example, one of the employees working as front-end development lead for the shopify.com web team owns Stiff Salt Co. along with his wife. Another employee Jane Lee also uses the platform to run her own business. She stated that "I joined really because it was so closely tied to my business. It helped me become an entrepreneur so much faster and helped me in so many ways." (as mentioned on the company's website). This philosophy is built into the culture at Shopify. Hiring for, and fostering entrepreneurship in every role has become a way to feed that passion back into the company itself. Shopify has an internal competition "Start your own business". On top of the standing $250 offer, all participating employees receive additional funding towards starting their own store. Further, the new business owners are connected to a mentorship program where they have access to experienced entrepreneur advisors. The winner is determined by who makes the most money and acknowledged within the company.

In their own words: When we are recruiting, we look for the candidates interested in solving the problems and challenges that we work with every day. The people that are curious and excited about finding solutions for problems are the people we want. We want people who are consumed by their craft and we want them to be entrepreneurial minded, running their own side hustles.

Things that make this approach awesome for the employees: There is lot of learning for employees. People are given the freedom to evolve their job roles and create their own opportunities. In the words of one of the employees that's one of the things Shopify is great for, there are so many doors you can open but you need to take the initiative. Employees are given flexibility to try different roles in the company. They can find what they love and pursue it to next level.

Things that make this approach awesome for the employer: Finding good talent is such a tough thing today, so it's extremely important to foster an environment that supports corporate entrepreneurship.

Results: This has helped Shopify to retain passionate people who are enthusiastic about the software product and exhibit product loyalty as well as can share their own entrepreneurship experiences with the customers. This has helped Shopify to build customer engagement and loyalty. Shopify has been able to unlock a dedication in its employee to its own product and attract passionate people.

Glassdoor Reviews of the company: Shopify is rated as 4.6/5 on Glassdoor. Of the 130 reviews on Glassdoor, 92% would recommend it to a friend and 96% approve of the CEO, Tobias Lutke.

(odynski, 2016) (Shopify, 2017) (Glassdoor, 2017)

Lockheed Corporation

What they do: Lockheed Martin Corporation, found in 1994, is a global security and aerospace company. It is engaged in the research, design, development, manufacture, integration and sustainment of advanced technology systems, products and services. The Company operates in five segments: Aeronautics; Information Systems & Global Solutions (IS&GS); Missiles and Fire Control (MFC); Mission Systems and Training (MST), and Space Systems. The Company provides a range of management, engineering, technical, scientific, logistics and information services. The Company's areas of focus are in defense, space, intelligence, homeland security and information technology, including cyber security. It serves customers, including military services, the United States Navy and various government agencies of the United States and other countries, as well as commercial and other customers.

Their approach to corporate entrepreneurship: Lockheed encourages intrapreneurs in their organization by giving them support and resources they need to thrive. They can define a clear path with their idea and they are given the power to modify and innovate as needed without any strict approval process. The best example is Lockheed Martin allowed Kelly Johnson to work as an autonomous organization with a small focused team. Kelly Johnson went on to form Skunk Works. Skunk Works developed some of the most innovative aircraft models including the SR71. One trick they applied to nurture the innovation-driven environment was to make them work in a space away from the regular corporate facility. Skunk Works worked out of a 'rented circus tent' - this was their secret laboratory/workshop in their beginning years. They value freedom from bureaucracy and allow innovators to transform their pet projects into small businesses without any recourse to the production, finance and marketing departments. They even allow a new project to start without a formal contract and without the formal written agreement.

In their own words: Skunk Works challenged the corporate 'red tape', broke official rules and was purely guided by intrapreneurship principles and 'out of the box' thinking. Kelly Johnson had put together the famous '14 Skunk Work Rules' for all Skunk Work employees:

The "Skunk Works®" manager must be delegated practically complete control of his program in all aspects. They should report to a division president or higher.

Strong but small project offices must be provided both by the military and industry.

The number of people having any connection with the project must be restricted in an almost vicious manner. Use a small number of good people (10% to 25% compared to the so-called normal systems).

A very simple drawing and drawing release system with great flexibility for making changes must be provided.

There must be a minimum number of reports required, but important work must be recorded thoroughly.

There must be a monthly cost review covering not only what has been spent and committed but also projected costs to the conclusion of the program. Don't have the books ninety days late and don't surprise the customer with sudden overruns.

The contractor must be delegated and must assume more than normal responsibility to get good vendor bids for subcontracts on the project. Commercial bid procedures are very often better than military ones.

The inspection system as currently used by ADP [Advanced Development Programs], which has been approved by both the Air Force and Navy, meets the intent of existing military requirements and should be used on new projects. Push more basic inspection responsibility back to subcontractors and vendors. Don't duplicate so much inspection.

The contractor must be delegated the authority to test their final product in flight. They can and must test it in the initial stages. If they don't, they rapidly lose their competency to design other vehicles.

The specifications applying to the hardware and software must be agreed to in advance of contracting. A specification section stating clearly which important military specification items will not knowingly be complied with and reasons is highly recommended.

Funding a program must be timely so that the contractor doesn't have to keep running to the bank to support government projects.

There must be mutual trust between the military project organization and the contractor with very close cooperation and liaison on a day-to-day basis. This cuts down misunderstanding and correspondence to an absolute minimum.

Access by outsiders to the project and its personnel must be strictly controlled by appropriate security measures.

Because only a few people will be used in engineering and most other areas, ways must be provided to reward good performance by pay not based on the number of personnel supervised.

Things that make this approach awesome for the employees: Employees enjoy the limitless opportunities to go beyond the traditional corporate boundaries for developing new products. During the process, they acquire new skill sets and become part of various intrapreneurial ventures.

Things that make this approach awesome for the employer: It helps the employer to remain competitive by pushing their boundaries and innovate.

Results: Intrapreneur Kelly Johnson and his "Skunk Works®" team designed and built the XP-80 in only 143 days (Seven days before the due day for delivery to ATSC.)

Glassdoor Reviews of the company: Lockheed is rated as 3.6/5 on Glassdoor. Of the 4353 reviews on Glassdoor, 73% would recommend it to a friend and 87% approve of the CEO, Merillyn Hewson.

(Haller, n.d.) (Lockheed, n.d.) (Abbie Griffin, 2014) (May, 2012) (Rainone, 2013) (Schlomo Maital, 2012) (Desouza, 2011)

Virgin

What they do: Virgin is an international investment group founded in 1970 with Sir Richard Branson. It has estimated revenue of $19.5 billion and a base of more than 71,000 employees. The Virgin Groups consists of over 60 businesses and serve nearly 60 million customers across the world. The company offers products and services in five core sectors including travel & leisure, financial services, health & wellness, telecoms and media, and music and entertainment. The group headquarters are in London, United Kingdom.

Their approach to corporate entrepreneurship: Sir Richard Branson places huge value on intrapreneurship. By adopting an intrapreneurship approach, Virgin has been able to launch numerous divisions e.g. airline, hotel, casino, books, music, megastore, mobile, wines, games and galactic. When the company had no prior experience in any of the new business areas, they would hire the best managers in that industry and then give them intrapreneurial freedom and empower them to set up their own ventures within the Virgin Group. Virgin's approach to corporate entrepreneurship is put across by Sir Richard Branson in this quote "We inadvertently developed this role at Virgin by virtue of the fact that when we've chosen to jump into a business about which we have little or no real knowledge, we've had to enable a few carefully selected people who do know which end is up." Employees can sidestep the organizational structures and bureaucratic processes to achieve the intrapreneurial goals. There are three hallmarks of intrapreneurship success in Virgin – freedom, empowerment and openness to innovation. Virgin's Intrapreneurship Program gets the total support from senior management and middle management for long-term success. Branson once said that one of the best things about this kind of intrapreneurship program at Virgin is that people become so immersed in what they are doing that they don't feel like they are working for someone.

In their own words: We wholeheartedly encourage our staff to be change agents and come up with ideas that improve not only our services and products, but also the way our people work. In fact, a thriving culture of intrapreneurship within the Group has led to some of the wonderful things that make Virgin stand out. Some of our companies have set up internal programs and hubs that encourage entrepreneurial thinking. In October 2014, Virgin Australia introduced the Ideas Lab to inspire team members to identify opportunities for innovation. Those that come up with outstanding concepts, which add value to the business, are crowned Innovation Champions. And the practice isn't just restricted to a few innovative thinkers; the Ideas Lab takes feedback from other staff members and posts challenges to get everyone thinking about entrepreneurial solutions. Some of the ideas that have been developed include new gate signage and different baggage delivery solutions. In fact, we encourage an open-door policy for innovation at all our businesses. Feedback forms, suggestion boxes, brainstorming meetings, and access to all levels of management inspire our people to speak up to turn challenges into opportunities. It's no surprise that so many of our employees go on to become entrepreneurs in their own right at some stage in the careers. Some companies don't like to encourage intrapreneurial thinking, worried that their staff might leave them to pursue a career elsewhere. Our mission is simple: we train our people well enough so they can leave, and treat them well enough so they don't want to. And if they do go off to do their own thing, we're absolutely delighted for them. Entrepreneurship is the cornerstone value of Virgin, so we couldn't be more proud of our staff that go on to pave their own path to business success.

Things that make this approach awesome for the employees: Employees learn a lot in this intrapreneurial culture. They experiment, learn from mistakes and go on to pave their own path either within or outside the company.

Things that make this approach awesome for the employer: Virgin is able to recruit the best employees by offering them intrapreneurial freedom and empowering them as corporate entrepreneurs (intrapreneurs) to "set up their own ventures within the Virgin Group." The stream of employees with intrapreneurial spirit has helped Virgin launch more than 200 Virgin companies.

Results: This out-of-the-box thinking is what has helped Virgin to grow into a 200-company strong empire. Intrapreneurs have helped the organization innovate and grow.

Glassdoor Reviews of the company: Virgin is rated as 2.6/5 on Glassdoor. Of the 7 reviews on Glassdoor, 44% would recommend it to a friend and 24% approve of the CEO, Richard Branson.

(Haller, Intrapreneurshipinstitute.com, n.d.) (Cook, 2015) (Deeb, 2015) (Glassdoor, 2017)

Apple

What they do: Apple Inc. is considered to be one of the most innovative companies of the world. Founded in 1977, Apple designs, manufactures and markets mobile communication, media devices, personal computers and portable digital music players. The company also sells a wide range of software services, accessories, networking solutions and third-party digital content and applications. iPhone, iPad, Mac, iPod, Apple Watch, Apple TV are among its leading products.

Their approach to corporate entrepreneurship: Apple believes that hierarchical structures thwart creativity and innovation in organization. Therefore, Apple has created autonomous startup-like teams in their organizations that can break free from organizational rigidity and think differently about important problems. Apple encourages democratic leadership culture instead of command style of leadership. In the early 1980's Steve Jobs and his handpicked group of twenty Apple Computer engineers separated themselves from the other Apple employees to innovatively and entrepreneurially create the Macintosh Computer (the "MAC"). This intrapreneurial group went on to become a "cult" within Apple Computer. Intrapreneurs can offer innovative ideas and work independently within the company. Apple fosters creativity within the work environment by giving the employees access and the ability to work amongst themselves. We trust people to take risks and push them to develop unique innovations. As Apple grew and became more bureaucratic, they created cultures that valued innovation and entrepreneurial thinking.

In their own words: Our tagline *Think Different* captures and reinforces our unique cult-like culture, the way we operate from top to bottom. Concepts like conventional wisdom and status quo don't exist at Apple headquarters in Cupertino. From the beginning, employees learn the Apple way: *Think Different*. It's not written anywhere and there are few processes to follow, but they learn it, just the same. And it works, big time. We empower our employees to make a difference. We give freedom and flexibility to our employees. People can come and go as they please if they accomplish not 100 per cent of our goals but 110 per cent. Like an employee says it's really fun place to work with loose rules. We have a specific group of employees called 'the creatives'. These are Apple's most valuable and productive employees specially cared for by our segmented and stratified organizational structure. We create teams that have a complementary mix of creative, proactive, visionary and opportunistic people, can produce ideas that are both innovative and actionable.

Things that make this approach awesome for the employees: Employees get a chance to collaborate across teams with different functions and enhance their skills. Intrapreneurs get to think and act like owners of the company, leverage internal resources, tap into best expertise to realize their innovative ideas.

Things that make this approach awesome for the employer: Apple takes calculated risk and plunges into promising markets or product lines. This helps to increase their market dominance. It has produced some of the most innovative products on the market and even launched whole new industries.

Results: Intrapreneurship helps Apple to stay fresh, relevant and ahead of competition. The company has come up with so many innovative products such as Apple Computer, Mac, iTune, iPad, iCloud, iPhone, Pixar etc.

Glassdoor Reviews of the company: Apple is rated as 4.0/5 on Glassdoor. Of the 8861 reviews on Glassdoor, 80% would recommend it to a friend and 94% approve of the CEO, Tim Cook.

(Haller, Steve Jobs the ultimate intrapreneur and entrepreneur, n.d.) (Pearce, 2014) (Tobak, 2011) (Samuel C. Certo, 1990) (Deloitte Digital, 2015) (Glassdoor.com, 2017)

Google

What they do: Google Inc. is a global technology company that designs and offers various products and services. The Company is primarily focused on web-based search and display advertising and tools, desktop and mobile operating systems, consumer content, enterprise solutions, commerce, and hardware products. In 2007 and 2008 Fortune Magazine named Google the Number 1 employer in their annual 100 best companies to work for. Google Inc. ranks #4 in FT Global 500 (2015).

Their approach to corporate entrepreneurship: Google encourages corporate entrepreneurship through implementing a formal program called '80/20 Innovation Time-Off (ITO) Model' in which employees are empowered to spend 20% of their work time (that is around 1 day per week) on projects that interest them and which they feel will benefit the company and its customers. The basic idea behind the Innovation Time-Off program is to foster creativity, innovation and out-of-the box thinking among its employees. It is a very successful program because it works from the bottom-up without any organizational bureaucracy and bottlenecks. This way good innovative ideas can spread fast, encourage collaboration, foster constructive input and minimize mistakes. It has a dedicated model of corporate entrepreneurship because the company provides funding and senior executive attention on prospective projects. When freed from the pressures of deadlines and targets, employees are said to be more creative.

In their own words: We empower our employees to do self-directed projects on company time with the idea that eventually their efforts will pay-off for the company. So long as the leader-directed projects are getting done on schedule, the employees and teams are free to expand Google's list of applications and features. As part of the program, employees form 'Google grouplets' comprised of engineers who share an interest in a novel idea, and aim to work on it to bring this idea into fruition.

Things that make this approach awesome for the employees: It is promising for the employees who are entrepreneurial in spirit but lack the resources to go out on their own. It gives employees the best of both the worlds – security of working for one of the most successful companies in the world alongside the platform to build their ideas.

Things that make this approach awesome for the employer: Almost half of Google products have been said to have emerged from this program. Google apps like Gmail, GoogleNews and AdSense are the list of successful products that came out of this innovation model.

It helps Google to recruit and retain some of the brightest creative minds.

Results: AdSense is now one of Google's most lucrative products earning $9.71 billion (28% of Google's total income) in 2011.

Glassdoor Reviews of the company: Google is rated as 4.4/5 on Glassdoor. Of the 6200 reviews on Glassdoor, 92% would recommend it to a friend and 97% approve of the CEO, Sundar Pichai.
(Haller H.) (Deeb, 2015)

W.L. Gore

What they do: W.L. Gore is a privately held American multinational in manufacturing and production industry and is based in Delaware. It is known amongst the "the world's most innovative companies". The company makes Gore-Tex water, windproof fabrics, synthetic vascular grafts, Elixir guitar strings and Glide dental floss. W.L. Gore is ranked as 159 on the Forbes' List of America's Largest Private Companies and ranked 43 on the Forbes' List of America's Best Employers. It has revenue of $2.9 billion and around 10,000 employees.

Their approach to corporate entrepreneurship: W.L. Gore is innovative in its operating principles. The company has a flat organizational structure with self-managed teams as the basic building blocks and no management layers. There are no job titles and employees refer to each other as associates. Job descriptions are also not fixed and specific roles and responsibilities are negotiated within the teams. Instead of job duties, people make commitments – they decide themselves where they can contribute the best. Operations are kept small and informal. They have a 'lattice' network structure where every individual is connected to every other in the organization. This results in free flow of information and a more personal level of communication. This enables cross-functional collaboration to be much easier. They believe that people are multi-faceted and so can't be expected to be 100% devoted to one thing at a time. Therefore, employees are allowed to work on two or three projects. Employees are allowed 10% of their work week free as " dabble time". During this time, they can choose any initiative and work on it. Someone who comes up with a breakthrough idea becomes a product champion. This product champion must convince other associates to rally a team for his or her project. If not enough people buy-in the idea and are ready to allocate their 'dabble time', that means the product champion's idea is not good enough. Only the ideas that are 'unique and valuable' and not "me too" ideas get ahead. After the "dabble time" is over, the product development team undergoes a three-stage cross-functional review process called "Real, Win, Worth." Questions like these are asked Is the opportunity real? Is there really somebody out there that will buy it? Can we win in the marketplace? What do the economics look like? Can we make money? Is it unique and valuable? Can we have a sustained advantage, say, patent protection? There is not time pressure put on the product champions. They get time to experiment, make mistakes and learn.

In their own words: One of our guiding principles is freedom for associates to achieve their own goals best by directing their efforts to the success of the corporation, to take action, to come up with ideas, to make mistakes as part of the creative process, to encourage each other to grow. We believe our employees to do what's right for the company and are culture is marked by fast decision making, diverse perspectives and collaboration of small teams.

Things that make this approach awesome for the employees: People enjoy the experience of working at W.L. Gore because they get opportunity to work on what they are passionate about, work in a collaborative environment and achieve their goals.

Things that make this approach awesome for the employer: W.L. Gore owes its success in product and market innovation to its evolving management model.

Results: Employee Dave Myers discovered that one of the company's products used for push-pull cables could be used to coat guitar strings for more comfortable strumming. W.L. Gore launched the guitar strings under the brand Elixir Strings, and they have become the front runner in the acoustic guitar string market.

Glassdoor Reviews of the company: W.L. Gore is rated as 3.0/5 on Glassdoor. Of the 459 reviews on Glassdoor, 54% would recommend it to a friend and 47% approve of the CEO, Terri Kelly.

(Haller H. , The WL Gore Success Story, n.d.) (Glassdoor, 2017)

Company: Shutterstock

What they do: Shutterstock is a New York-based company founded in 2003. It is a leading provider of high-quality licensed photographs, vectors, illustrations, videos and music to businesses, marketing agencies and media organizations around the world. The company has offices in Amsterdam, Berlin, Chicago, Denver, London, Paris and San Francisco. It has a customer base spread across 150 countries and a growing community of more than 60,000 contributors. The company also owns Bigstock, a value-oriented stock media agency; Offset, a high-end image collection; Skillfeed, an online marketplace for learning; and WebDAM, a cloud-based digital asset management service for businesses.

Their approach to corporate entrepreneurship: Shutterstock does not have strict hierarchies and closed-door policies. It gives freedom to its employees to pursue their entrepreneurial passions. Being entrepreneurial at Shutterstock means 'creative, resourceful and unafraid to fail'. This has helped to foster an innovation culture in the organization. Every year, Shutterstock hosts an annual hackathon which is 24-hour brainstorming challenge to produce brilliant, innovative ideas on how can the company serve its customers better. Before each hackathon, employees take the time to research the market, test ideas and fix potential glitches. They are then given extra 4 hours to make their demo presentation. They allow their employees to take risks and work on projects they are passionate about.

In their own words: As put by Jon Oringer, Founder, Chairman and CEO of Shutterstock "We encourage everyone to be entrepreneurial. We do have a big company vision so you can't just do whatever you want ... [but] it's important that we have people that are constructively disruptive just like we were on day one. We strive to maintain a culture of openness, listening and innovation. We listen to employees and customers, and encourage them to contribute their own ideas. You need to constantly be listening and on the lookout for this stuff, and if you set up the organization and the culture right, these ideas will bubble up, and people will be talking about them and people should feel that they're free to talk about them.

Things that make this approach awesome for the employees: Creative people get the freedom to pursue their creative passions within the company and increase their job satisfaction.

Things that make this approach awesome for the employer: The company can retain the most talented individuals as well as experiment with new product ideas that can keep their customers happier and loyal, increase revenue and improve business processes.

Results: Some of the innovative products of Shutterstock such as Spectrum and Oculus sprouted up in the hackathons. In the last two years, Shutterstock has also launched two other businesses – Offset which provides high-end imagery, and Skillfeed which is a marketplace of online learning.

Glassdoor Reviews of the company: Shutterstock is rated as 3.5/5 on Glassdoor. Of the 129 reviews on Glassdoor, 57% would recommend it to a friend and 66% approve of the CEO, Jon Oringer.

(Evans, 2014) (Gaskell, 2016) (Howard, 2015) (Glassdoor, 2016)

Company: Texas Instruments

What they do: Texas Instruments (TI) is an American semi-conductor components innovator and manufacturer based in Dallas, Texas. It designs, makes and sells semiconductors to electronics designers and manufacturers across the world. The company operates through two segments: Analog and Embedded Processing. The Company has operations in over 30 countries.

Their approach to corporate entrepreneurship: Texas Instruments encourages its engineers to have an intrapreneurial mindset. The company has an intrapreneurship program called IDEA which stands for identify, develop, expose and action. This program is open to all employees and offers seed funding of $25,000 to develop promising concepts in their very early stages, before they qualify for R&D funding. TI Registration and Identification System (TIRIS) is one of the most successful projects to come out of IDEA. Within the company, there is a technical ladder which encourages small teams of intrapreneurs to work on their creative ideas and match engineers with great ideas to design products that can make a huge business impact. At Texas Instruments, idea generators are called 'lunatics' because they are the people who think outside the box and look beyond the challenges and see the future possibilities and potential. They are likely to be the dreamers who may not excel at routine tasks but are obsessed with seeking answers to a problem. Texas Instrument allows its employees to take on the role of a dreamer and to allocate a part of their work time to pursue projects with no specific goals in sight and which can be considered risky. At Texas Instruments, when engineers get excited about a technological problem, they are often given free-time to pursue it. The path to innovation is kept open without any interference from the marketing department to scrutinize the idea. If the employee can identify a sponsor and get an approval, then there is an opportunity to develop it. The intrapreneurship strategy of the company is to allow idea creators to pursue their ideas for their own sake, not just to seek economic benefits out of it. The focus is on value creation not on the economic outcomes.

In their own words: We give our people both autonomy and accountability. They are empowered to innovate more as they produce better and better results

Things that make this approach awesome for the employees: It is not just challenging but a rewarding experience for young engineers.

Things that make this approach awesome for the employer: Texas Instruments studied 50 of its successful and unsuccessful new product efforts. In each of the successes there was at least one dedicated intrapreneurs who persisted despite great obstacles. Conversely, the common denominator of the failures was the absence of a zealous volunteer champion.

Results: Texas Instruments has developed some of the major innovations that have shaped the modern electronics industry. Notable ones are transistor radio, integrated circuit, microprocessor, handheld calculator, digital light processing, single-chip digital signal processor and many more.

Glassdoor Reviews of the company: Texas Instruments is rated as 4.0/5 on Glassdoor. Of the 1722 reviews on Glassdoor, 85% would recommend it to a friend and 92%approve of the CEO, Rich Templeton.

(Madigan, 1998) (Desouza, 2011) (Pinchot, 1986) (Glassdoor, 2017)

How do you know when it's the right time to quit your day job?

The folks at Infusionsoft have a useful infographic that breaks down quite nicely the stages of small businesses and approximates the revenue you should be making before you quit your day job. Basically, depending on your stage in life once your side hustle is making between 4-10k monthly you might be in a position to quit your day job.

Visit: http://www.sidehustlenation.com/companies-that-encourage-employees-to-side-hustle/

Signs you are ready to quit your day job

1. You have run the numbers and the math makes sense. For example, you are making enough to sustain your expenses and you have a business plan that reasonably projects sustainable growth. And you have saved a decent buffer of capital to give you some runway as your transition away from a steady paycheck.

2. You feel 100% committed to your side business and it is evident in your actions as you continue to dedicate time to your side business. Your belief and excitement continues to grow instead of waning with time and you are ready to face the fear of uncertainty head-on.

3. Your 7pm-12 mid-night job is starting to feel like a 9-5 in-terms of the volume of work and you are at the stage where one has to go.

4. You have customers or clients that love you and talk about it. When you start getting press mentions and social validation it's usually a good sign that you are onto something worth pursuing.

5. You have a diversified set of skills, tools and resources that can sustain you until the time you are ready to take on employees to enable you to scale.

With these factors in place you may indeed be ready to quit your job and cross over to being an entrepreneur. You may be ready to start your journey to building a corporation. Hopefully you are armed with experience and skills you learned to be an intrapreneurial employee in a corporation and have an edge that will aid in your success and ability to sustain beyond being a successful startup. How can we measure whether we can do better than 10% and improve the 90% tech startup or 50% small business failure rate? I don't have an answer except to hope that some of you will take up the call to action below. There will be some who will vigorously defend the opinion that entrepreneurship is in your DNA and they may very well be right. I simply believe that that entrepreneurship can be nurtured in a corporation in the right environment. I also believe that there are some who leap too soon to the startup world without building some chops they will need to lead a sustainable business. Corporations are successful startups and it stands to reason that there will be something to learn from them. If there was a Crushing Corporate hall of fame it would probably have two categories.

1. Leaders who are successfully leading 20+ year old corporations
2. Leaders who have founded disruptive new companies

I value both these categories because they each have their own set of challenges and management skills needed to win and if you are an employee there are opportunities to drive business growth, innovation and professional skill growth in both scenarios. Let people like Jay-z, Oprah, Gary Vaynerchuk, Howard Shultz, Ken Chenault, Sarah Blakely, Jeff Bezos, Tory Burch and operators like Eric Schmidt and Sheryl Sandberg all inspire you with the various ways corporate experience has helped them in their entrepreneurial journey

The call to action of this book is simple:

1. Spend enough time crushing corporate at least 2-3 years
2. Embrace intrapreneurship while at the corporation and learn everything you can.

3. Use the tools suggested in the 4 R's Reputation, Reality, Risks and Rewards to build a foundation that will ensure that you can give entrepreneurship a real effort.

4. Remember that startups are not built on their own so when you seek to emulate successful founders and read their stories beyond the headline and broaden your scope to understand the operators they surrounded themselves with and the role corporate experience has played in getting a business from startup to a corporation.

Having read the book, you can now define Crushing Corporate as a change in perspective and mindset that allows you to:

- Learn everything you need to know about how companies work to make yourself a better operator as an entrepreneur.

- Use the time at the corporation to do big things that will drive credibility and justify you highlighting your experience when you seek investment for a venture or join a startup.

- Find ideas at the corporation that could become businesses or services in and of themselves.

- Use your time at corporations to find your potential co-founder, business partner or ultimate customer.

- Learn and gain foundational business skills

- Discover and hone your strengths

- A way to build credibility and earn respect in your field

Bibliography

3M. (2002). *A Century of Innovation.* Retrieved from multimedia.3m.com: http://multimedia.3m.com/mws/media/171240O/3m-coi-book-tif.pdf

Abbie Griffin, c. N. (2014). *Open Innovation: New Product Development Essentials from the PDMA .* John Wiley & sons.

Aristotle. (340 BC). *Teachings.* Stagira: Self Published.

basecamp.com. (1999). *About.* Retrieved from Basecamp.com: https://basecamp.com/about

Beda, A. (2011, September 23). *A 15% Time For Employees To Develop Own Projects Called The"Bootlegging".* Retrieved from Intrapreneurshipconference.com: https://www.intrapreneurshipconference.com/bootlegging/

Beda, A. (2011, October 12). *Sony Playstation an Intrapreneurship Story.* Retrieved from Intrapreneurshipconference.com: https://www.intrapreneurshipconference.com/sony-playstation-true-intrapreneurship/

Bihr, P. (2008, march 6). *How to create the best workplace? Ask 37signals.* Retrieved from thewavingcat.com: https://www.thewavingcat.com/tag/37signals/

Boris Groysberg, A. N. (2006, May). *HBR.* Retrieved from HBR.org: https://hbr.org/2006/05/are-leaders-portable

Boyatzis, D. G. (2017, February 6). *Emotional Intelligence has 12 elements. Which do you need to work on?* Retrieved from HBR.org: https://hbr.org/2017/02/emotional-intelligence-has-12-elements-which-do-you-need-to-work-on

Caligiuri, R. (2015, April 28). *Three lessons on innovation from Basecamp.* Retrieved from theglobeandmail.com:

http://www.theglobeandmail.com/report-on-business/small-business/three-lessons-on-innovation-from-basecamp/article24136130/

CCSBE. (1996). Journal of Small Business and Entrepreneurship. Vol. 13, No. 2. *Journal of Small Business and Entrepreneurship. Vol. 13, No. 2*, 2.

Clifford, C. (2013, October 17). *Keep Your Employees Loyal By Encouraging Them to Pursue Their Own Projects and Passions.* Retrieved from Entrepreneur.com: https://www.entrepreneur.com/article/229416

Coffey, B. (2011, August 23). *Combating the innovators dilemma.* Retrieved from Onstartups.com: http://onstartups.com/tabid/3339/bid/64449/Combating-the-Innovators-Dilemma-HubSpot-s-Experiments-Framework.aspx

Cook, P. (2015, February 3). *How to break down barriers and allow intrapreneurs to flourish.* Retrieved from Virgin.com: https://www.virgin.com/entrepreneur/how-to-break-down-the-barriers-and-allow-intrapreneurs-to-flourish

Csikszentmihalyi, M. (2004, February). *Flow the secret to hapiness.* Retrieved from TED.com: https://www.ted.com/talks/mihaly_csikszentmihalyi_on_flow

Cuban, M. (2007). *blogmaverick.com.* Retrieved from Why I dont wear a suit and cant figure out why anyonne does: http://blogmaverick.com/2007/01/16/why-i-dont-wear-a-suit-and-cant-figure-out-why-anyone-does/

Deeb, G. (2015, March 19). *Bid compnaies that ebmrace intrapreneurship will thrive.* Retrieved from Entrepreneur.com: https://www.entrepreneur.com/article/243884

Deloitte Digital. (2015). *5 Insights into Intrapreneurship.* Retrieved from Deloitte.com: https://www2.deloitte.com/content/dam/Deloitte/de/Documents/technology/Intrapreneurship_Whitepaper_English.pdf

Derek Lehmberg, W. G. (2009, January). *GENERAL ELECTRIC: AN OUTLIER IN CEO TALENT DEVELOPMENT.* Retrieved from iveybusinessjournal.com: http://iveybusinessjournal.com/publication/general-electric-an-outlier-in-ceo-talent-development/

Desouza, K. C. (2011). *Intrapreneurship: Managing Ideas within your organization.* University of Toronto Press.

Digman, L. A. (1997). *Strategic Management: concepts, processes and decisions. .* Dame Publications.

Edmonson, A. C. (2011, April). *Strategies for learning from failure.* Retrieved from HBR.org: https://hbr.org/2011/04/strategies-for-learning-from-failure

Edwards, D. (2015, October 14). *The hard thing about intrapreneurship.* Retrieved from Linkedin.com/pulse: https://www.linkedin.com/pulse/hard-thing-intrapreneurship-dougal-edwards

Emmanuel, M. (2010). *Methodology of Business Studies.* Pearson Education.

Esteban R. Brenes, J. H. (2012). *The Future of Entrepreneurship in Latin American.* Palgrave Macmilla.

Evans, L. (2014, April 22). *How intrapreneurship encouraged shutterstocks creative success.* Retrieved from Fastcompany.com: https://www.fastcompany.com/3029344/bottom-line/how-intrapreneurship-encouraged-shutterstocks-creative-success

Ferrier, A. (2014, April 23). *Innovation Networks In Action – An Intuit Case Study.* Retrieved from Culturevate.com: http://www.culturevate.com/intuit-case-study/

Fried, J. (2008, March 5). *Workplace Experiements.* Retrieved from signalnoise.com: https://signalvnoise.com/posts/893-workplace-experiments

Gall, S. (2006, November 14). *Examples of Intrapreneural Success.* Retrieved from stevegall.wikifoundry.com: http://stevegall.wikifoundry.com/page/Entrepreneurship

Gaskell, A. (2016, December 2). *The power of Intrapreneurship in driving Innovation.* Retrieved from Forbes: http://www.forbes.com/sites/adigaskell/2016/12/02/the-power-of-intrapreneurship-in-driving-innovation/#55213de51007

George, D. (2016, february 18). *Big companies must embrace intrapreneurship to survive.* Retrieved from Forbes.com: http://www.forbes.com/sites/georgedeeb/2016/02/18/big-companies-must-embrace-intrapreneurship-to-survive/#30ee450feb9e

Glassdoor. (2016, December 2). *Shutterstock Reviews.* Retrieved from Glassdoor.com: https://www.glassdoor.co.in/Reviews/Shutterstock-Reviews-E270840.htm

Glassdoor. (2017). *3M reviews.* Retrieved from Glassdoor.com: https://www.glassdoor.com/Reviews/3M-Reviews-E446.htm

Glassdoor. (2017, February). *Facebook Reviews.* Retrieved from Glassdoor.com: https://www.glassdoor.co.in/Reviews/Facebook-Reviews-E40772.htm

Glassdoor. (2017, February). *General Motors Reviews*. Retrieved from Glassdoor: https://www.glassdoor.com/Reviews/General-Motors-Reviews-E279.htm

Glassdoor. (2017, February). *Hubspot Reviews*. Retrieved from Glassdoor.com: https://www.glassdoor.com/Reviews/HubSpot-Reviews-E227605.htm

Glassdoor. (2017, February). *Infusionsoft Reviews*. Retrieved from Glassdoor.com: https://www.glassdoor.com/Reviews/Infusionsoft-Reviews-E332306.htm

Glassdoor. (2017, February 10). *Inutit Reviews*. Retrieved from Glassdoor.com: https://www.glassdoor.co.in/Reviews/Intuit-Reviews-E2293.htm

Glassdoor. (2017, February). *Shopify Reviews*. Retrieved from Shopify: https://www.glassdoor.com/Reviews/Shopify-Reviews-E675933.htm

Glassdoor. (2017, February). *Sony Reviews*. Retrieved from Glassdoor.com: https://www.glassdoor.com/Reviews/Sony-Reviews-E3541.htm

Glassdoor. (2017). *Sun Microsystems Reviews*. Retrieved from Glassdoor.com: https://www.glassdoor.com/Reviews/Sun-Microsystems-Reviews-E1924.htm

Glassdoor. (2017, February). *Texas Instruments Reviews*. Retrieved from Glassdoor.com: https://www.glassdoor.com/Reviews/Texas-Instruments-Reviews-E651.htm

Glassdoor. (2017, February). *Virgin Reviews*. Retrieved from Glassdoor.com:

https://www.glassdoor.co.uk/Reviews/Virgin-Group-Reviews-E3428.htm

Glassdoor. (2017, February). *W L Gore Reviews*. Retrieved from Glassdoor.com: https://www.glassdoor.com/Reviews/W-L-Gore-Reviews-E3044.htm

Glassdoor. (2017, February). *Working at Basecamp*. Retrieved from Glassdoor: https://www.glassdoor.com/Overview/Working-at-BaseCamp-Data-Solutions-EI_IE575424.11,34.htm

Glassdoor.com. (2017, February). *Apple Reviews*. Retrieved from Glassdoor.com: https://www.glassdoor.com/Reviews/Apple-Reviews-E1138.htm

Goleman, D. (2012). *Emotional Intelligence*. Bantam.

Griffith, E. (2016, December 28th). *The Ugly Unethical Underside of Silicon Valley*. Retrieved from Fortune.com: http://fortune.com/silicon-valley-startups-fraud-venture-capital/?xid=for_em_sh

Halladay, H. (2011, March). *How to hire a dream manager for your small business*. Retrieved from Learn.infusionsoft.com: https://learn.infusionsoft.com/growth/personal-development/dream-manager-for-small-business

Haller, H. E. (n.d.). Retrieved from Intrapreneurshipinstitute.com: http://www.intrapreneurshipinstitute.com/intrapreneurship-case-studies/sir-richard-branson-successful-multi-billionaire-entrepreneur-supports-and-uses-intrapreneurship/

Haller, H. E. (n.d.). *Lockheed Skunk works Intrapreneurship in action*. Retrieved from Intrapreneurshipinstitute.com: http://www.intrapreneurshipinstitute.com/intrapreneurship-case-studies/lockheed-skunk-works-intrapreneurship-in-action/

Haller, H. E. (n.d.). *Steve Jobs the ultimate intrapreneur and entrepreneur*. Retrieved from intrapreneurshipinstitute.com: http://www.intrapreneurshipinstitute.com/intrapreneurship-case-studies/steve-jobs-the-ultimate-intrapreneur-and-entrepreneur/

Haller, H. (n.d.). *Googles Entrepreneurship Program*. Retrieved from intrapreneurshipinstitute.com: http://www.intrapreneurshipinstitute.com/intrapreneurship-case-studies/intrapreneurship-case-study-googles-intrapreneurship-program-is-very-successful/

Haller, H. (n.d.). *The WL Gore Success Story*. Retrieved from selfgrowth.com: http://www.selfgrowth.com/articles/intrapreneurship_succe ss_the_wl_gore_success_story_overviewHoward

HBR. (2016, April). *How Intuit built a better support system for intrapreneurs*. Retrieved from HBR.org: https://hbr.org/2016/04/how-intuit-built-a-better-support-system-for-intrapreneurs

Howard, B. (2015). *We-Commerce: How to Create, Collaborate, and Succeed in the Sharing Economy*. Penguin.

Hurst, A. (2015). *The Purpose Economy*. Elevate.

Ian Marcouse, N. W. (2015). *AQA Business for A Level* . Hachette. Retrieved from AQA Business for A Level (Marcousé) by Ian Marcouse, Nigel Watson, and Andrew Hammond. Hachette UK (2015).

Imposter Phenomenon. (1978). Retrieved from PaulineRoseClance.com: http://paulineroseclance.com/impostor_phenomenon.html

Infusionsoft. (2017). *Culture*. Retrieved from Infusionsoft.com: https://www.infusionsoft.com/about/culture

Intuit. (2009). *Innovation Catalysts*. Retrieved from IntuitLabs.com: http://www.intuitlabs.com/innovationcatalysts/

Jonas, C. (2016, July). *5 strategies to attract and retain top talent.* Retrieved from crystaljonas.com: http://crystaljonas.com/wp-content/uploads/2016/07/5-Strategies-to-Attract-and-Retain-Top-Talent.pdf

Kali Fry. (2015, September 23). *Intrapreneurs ignite internal innovation.* Retrieved from Intuitlabs.com: http://www.intuitlabs.com/blog/intrapreneurs-ignite-internal-innovation/

Kneece, R. (2014, September 17). *10 inspiring examples of successful intrapreneurship.* Retrieved from insights.wired.com: http://insights.wired.com/profiles/blogs/10-inspiring-examples-of-successful-intrapreneurship#axzz4W6AoWtRG

Kurtz., L. E. (2011). *Contemporary Business* . John Wiley and Sons . Retrieved from Contemporary Business by Louis E. Boone and David L. Kurtz. John Wiley and Sons (2011)

Leow, D. (2016). *The Asian Millenial Workforce and the Travel Industry.* Singapore Tourism Board.

Leslie, R. (2006, November 25). *Promise Not to Call.* Retrieved from Youtube: https://youtu.be/FS-3dNPOin0

Leslie, R. (2008, April 27). *Ryan Leslie Makes Addiction.* Retrieved from Youtube: https://youtu.be/-Ix5dicdL7c

Lockheed. (n.d.). *Kellys 14 rules and practices.* Retrieved from lockheedmartin.com: http://lockheedmartin.com/us/aeronautics/skunkworks/14rules.html

Loper, N. (2015, April 13). *sidehustlenation.com.* Retrieved from 5 Companies That Encourage Their Employees to Side Hustle:

http://www.sidehustlenation.com/companies-that-encourage-employees-to-side-hustle/

Loudon, A. (2001). *Webs of Innovation: The Networked Economy Demands New Ways to Innovate* . FT.com.

Lussier, R. N. (2014). *Management Fundamentals: Concepts, Applications and Skill Development* . Sage Publications.

Madigan, C. O. (1998, October 1). *Agents of Innovation.* Retrieved from businessfinancemag.com: http://businessfinancemag.com/hr/agents-innovation

Magida, J. (2012, June 25). *Intrapreneurship what who and why it's important.* Retrieved from ischool.syr.edu: https://ischool.syr.edu/infospace/2012/06/25/intrapreneursh ip-what-who-and-why-its-important/

May, M. E. (2012, October 9). *The rules of successful skunk works projects.* Retrieved from fastcompany.com: https://www.fastcompany.com/3001702/rules-successful-skunk-works-projects

Mayberry, M. (2015, November 20). *Why every company needs a dream manager.* Retrieved from Entrepreneur.com: https://www.entrepreneur.com/article/253067

McNealy, R. E. (2011). *The Innovation Catalysts.* Retrieved from HBR.org: https://hbr.org/2011/06/the-innovation-catalysts

Morgan, J. (2015, December 14). *How Infusionsoft uses culture as thier greatest competitive advantage.* Retrieved from Forbes.com: http://www.forbes.com/sites/jacobmorgan/2015/12/14/how -infusionsoft-uses-culture-as-their-greatest-competitive-advantage/#159bf30d70d1

My-personality-test.com. (2016, December). Retrieved from My-personality-test.com: http://www.my-personality-test.com/

odynski, M. (2016, July 13). *How Shopify sharpens its platform hire your customers*. Retrieved from techvibes.com: https://techvibes.com/2016/07/13/shopify-platform-hire-customers

Oetting, J. (2015, April 21). *How to start a startup inside your agency*. Retrieved from blog.hubspot.com: https://blog.hubspot.com/agency/startup-inside-agency#sm.000001o04mipejebprbo6feh3u8qt

Pearce, K. (2014, May 16). *THE ENTREPRENEURSHIP MINDSET: FREELANCERS, INTRAPRENEURS AND STARTUP CULTURE*. Retrieved from diygenius.com: https://www.diygenius.com/the-entrepreneurship-mindset/

Pedram Keyani. (2012, May 23). *Stay focused and keep hacking*. Retrieved from facebook.com: https://www.facebook.com/notes/facebook-engineering/stay-focused-and-keep-hacking/10150842676418920/

Phillips, G. D. (2007). *Managing Now*. Cengage Learning.

Pinchot, G. (1986). *Intrapreneuring*. Harper & Row.

Rainone, M. (2013, July). *How to build and Intrapreneurial Organization*. Retrieved from pddnet.com: https://www.pddnet.com/blog/2013/07/how-build-intrapreneurial-organization

Richards, C. (2015, October 26). *Learning to deal with the imposter syndrome*. Retrieved from nytimes.com: https://www.nytimes.com/2015/10/26/your-money/learning-to-deal-with-the-impostor-syndrome.html?_r=2

Rosenberg, M. (2003). *Non-Violent Communication - The Language of Life*. PuddleDancer Press.

Sahadi, J. (2015, April 27). *4 Day work week*. Retrieved from money.cnn.com: http://money.cnn.com/2015/04/27/pf/4-day-work-week/

Samuel C. Certo, F. M. (1990). *Business by Samuel C. Certo, F. Michael Kaufmann, Stewart W. Husted, James B. Pettijohn, Max E. Douglas. Allyn and Bacon (1990). S.* Allyn and Bacon . Retrieved from Business by Samuel C. Certo, F. Michael Kaufmann, Stewart W. Husted, James B. Pettijohn, Max E. Douglas. Allyn and Bacon (1990). .

Schawbel, D. (2012, July 29). *How big companies are becoming entrepreneurial.* Retrieved from Techcrunch.com: https://techcrunch.com/2012/07/29/how-big-companies-are-becoming-entrepreneurial/

Schawbel, D. (2013, September 3). Retrieved from Entrepreneur.com:
https://www.entrepreneur.com/article/227725

Schawbel, D. (2013, september 3). Retrieved from https://www.entrepreneur.com/article/227725

Schawbel, D. (2013, September 3). *Why companies want you to become an intrapreneur.* Retrieved from Forbes.com: http://www.forbes.com/sites/danschawbel/2013/09/09/why-companies-want-you-to-become-an-intrapreneur/#18e8ac4624d3

Schlomo Maital, D. S. (2012). *Innovation Management: Strategies, Concepts, and Tools for Growth and Profits.* Sage Publications.

Shopify. (2017, February). *Careers.* Retrieved from Shopify.com: https://www.shopify.com/careers

Sinek, S. (2009). *Start With Why.* Penguin.

Socrates. (430 BC). *Musings.* Ahtens: Self Published.

Swearingen, J. (2008, June 17). *Great Intrapreneurs in Business History*. Retrieved from cbsnews.com: http://www.cbsnews.com/news/great-intrapreneurs-in-business-history/

Tobak, S. (2011, March). *10 ways to think different inside Apples cult like culture*. Retrieved from cbsnews.com: http://www.cbsnews.com/news/10-ways-to-think-different-inside-apples-cult-like-culture/

Tobias, J. (2016, February). *Intuit sparks startu up fire in its employees*. Retrieved from InnovationExcellence.com: http://innovationexcellence.com/blog/2016/02/03/intuit-sparks-start-up-fire-in-its-employees/

Upbin, B. (2012, september 12). *Why Intuit is more Innovative than your company*. Retrieved from Forbes.com: http://www.forbes.com/sites/bruceupbin/2012/09/04/intuit-the-30-year-old-startup/#6bbe45855b83

Vocoli. (2014, May 27). *10 Inspiring examples of successful intrapreneurship*. Retrieved from Vocoli: https://www.vocoli.com/blog/may-2014/10-inspiring-examples-of-successful-intrapreneurship/

Vozza, S. (2015, June 17). *How companies actually make four day workweeks feasible*. Retrieved from fastcompany.com: https://www.fastcompany.com/3047329/the-future-of-work/how-companies-actually-make-four-day-workweeks-feasible

Wagner, G. (2016, March). *Role Models for Whole Person Organizational Cultures*. Retrieved from Culturerolemodels.com: http://culturerolemodels.com/march-april-2016.html

White, C. (2004). *Strategic Management* . Palgrave Macmillan.

Wise, B. F. (2015). *Startup Opportunities: Know when to quit your day job.* FG Press.

Yoon, E. (2015, July). *Why Marketing needs more introverts.* Retrieved from HBR.org: https://hbr.org/2014/07/why-marketing-needs-more-introverts

Young, V. (2011). *The Secret thoughts of Successful Women.* Crown Publishing.

Zook, C. (2016, December 27). *When Large Companies Are Better at Entrepreneurship than Startups.* Retrieved from HBR.org: https://hbr.org/2016/12/when-large-companies-are-better-at-entrepreneurship-than-startups

Index

ABOUT THE AUTHOR

FREE Career Chats Weekly
Text "Crushing" to (646) 762-9411
CRUSHINGCORPORATE.COM
Linkedin.com/in/yolichisholm

Yoli Chisholm has a passion for the impact of culture as a lever to optimize business performance. We were first introduced to her thinking with her 2013 TEDx Talk "Are you a strong tree" which was well received with over 25,000 views. Currently Yoli Chisholm is a Senior Director at Microsoft and debuts as an author with Crushing Corporate where she makes the case for the value of taking that corporate job before you venture into entrepreneurship. She has a 20-year record of corporate entrepreneurship having worked for Fortune 100 companies like Microsoft as well as startups that have grown to corporations like eBay, Points.com and Lavalife.com. Yoli has crossed industries from technology, retail, healthcare, dating, travel to tele-communications in multiple markets Canada, United States, South Africa. Her book Crushing Corporate asks the reader "What if instead of pushing people to become entrepreneurs first, we enabled professionals to be better intrapreneurs – would the results be more successful entrepreneurs? Is the negative narrative on working for a corporation doing wannabe entrepreneurs a dis-service? Can we do better than the current startup success rate?

Made in the USA
San Bernardino, CA
24 February 2017